Devil's Advocates

DEVIL'S ADVOCATES is a series of books devoted to exploring the classics of horror cinema. Contributors to the series come from the fields of teaching, academia, journalism and fiction, but all have one thing in common: a passion for the horror film and a desire to share it with the widest possible audience.

'The admirable Devil's Advocates series is not only essential – and fun – reading for the serious horror fan but should be set texts on any genre course.'
Dr Ian Hunter, Reader in Film Studies, De Montfort University, Leicester

'Auteur Publishing's new Devil's Advocates critiques on individual titles… offer bracingly fresh perspectives from passionate writers. The series will perfectly complement the BFI archive volumes.' **Christopher Fowler,** *Independent on Sunday*

'Devil's Advocates has proven itself more than capable of producing impassioned, intelligent analyses of genre cinema… quickly becoming the go-to guys for intelligent, easily digestible film criticism.' **Horror Talk.com**

'Auteur Publishing continue the good work of giving serious critical attention to significant horror films.' **Black Static**

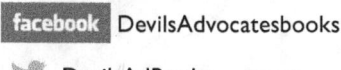 DevilsAdvocatesbooks

DevilsAdBooks

Also available in this series

A Girl Walks Home Alone at Night Farshid Kazemi
Black Sunday Martyn Conterio
The Blair Witch Project Peter Turner
Blood and Black Lace Roberto Curti
The Blood on Satan's Claw David Evans-Powell
Candyman Jon Towlson
Cannibal Holocaust Calum Waddell
Cape Fear Rob Daniel
Carrie Neil Mitchell
The Company of Wolves James Gracey
The Conjuring Kevin J. Wetmore Jr.
Creepshow Simon Brown
Cruising Eugenio Ercolani & Marcus Stiglegger
The Curse of Frankenstein Marcus K. Harmes
Daughters of Darkness Kat Ellinger
Dawn of the Dead Jon Towlson
Dead of Night Jez Conolly & David Bates
The Descent James Marriot
The Devils Darren Arnold
Don't Look Now Jessica Gildersleeve
The Evil Dead Lloyd Haynes
The Fly Emma Westwood
Frenzy Ian Cooper
Halloween Murray Leeder
House of Usher Evert Jan van Leeuwen
In the Mouth of Madness Michael Blyth
IT Chapters One and Two Alissa Burger
It Follows Joshua Grimm
Ju-on The Grudge Marisa Hayes
Let the Right One In Anne Billson
M Samm Deighan
Macbeth Rebekah Owens
The Mummy Doris V. Sutherland
Nosferatu Cristina Massaccesi
The Omen Adrian Schober
Peeping Tom Kiri Bloom Walden
Pet Sematary Shellie McMurdo
Possession Alison Taylor
Re-Animator Eddie Falvey
Repulsion Jeremy Carr
Saw Benjamin Poole
Scream Steven West
The Shining Laura Mee
Shivers Luke Aspell
The Silence of the Lambs Barry Forshaw
Suspiria Alexandra Heller-Nicholas
The Texas Chain Saw Massacre James Rose
The Thing Jez Conolly
Trouble Every Day Kate Robertson
Twin Peaks: Fire Walk With Me Lindsay Hallam
Witchfinder General Ian Cooper

Forthcoming

The Craft Miranda Corcoran
Poltergeist Rob McLaughlin

Devil's Advocates

The Cabin in the Woods

Susanne Kord

First published in 2023 by
Auteur, an imprint of
Liverpool University Press,
4 Cambridge Street,
Liverpool
L69 7ZU

This paperback edition published 2025

Series design: Nikki Hamlett at Cassels Design
Set by Carnegie Book Production, Lancaster

All rights reserved. No part of this publication may be reproduced in any material form (including photocopying or storing in any medium by electronic means and whether or not transiently or incidentally to some other use of this publication) without the permission of the copyright owner.

British Library Cataloguing-in-Publication Data
A catalogue record for this book is available from the British Library
ISBN hardback: 978-1-80085-644-8
ISBN paperback: 978-1-83624-403-5
ISBN PDF: 978-1-80085-520-5

Contents

Figures vii

Chapter 1: Into the Woods: Introduction 1

Chapter 2: Fealty v. Nihilism: How (Not) to Save the World 23

Chapter 3: Either v. Or: The Puppets' Choice 47

Chapter 4: Alignment v. Allegiance: How We See 63

Chapter 5: Guilt v. Fear: Why We Look 83

Bibliography / Filmography 101

Figures

Figure 1. Theatrical release poster for *The Cabin in the Woods* (2012) 2

Figures 2–4. Look-alike cabins in *The Cabin in the Woods*, *The Evil Dead* and *Cabin Fever* 10

Figure 5. Dana in the cabin's crosshairs 30

Figure 6. Dana explores the cabin 31

Figure 7. Marty contemplates the woods 31

Figure 8. Patience Buckner to the rescue 39

Figure 9. Dana as an invitation to 'transgress' 53

Figure 10. Holden as an invitation to 'transgress' 53

Figure 11. The Downstairs crew anticipate the unbuttoning of a blouse 58

Figure 12. Hadley and Sitterson anticipate the unbuttoning of a blouse 58

Figure 13. Jules, her attacker and her protectors 71

Figures 14–16. Pieces of Jules 72

Figure 17. Focusing on the details: tongues 73

Figure 18. Focusing on the details: butt 74

Figure 19. Dana looks at the last piece of Jules 74

Figure 20. *Cabin*'s image gallery of horrors 78

Figure 21. The single image 79

Figure 22. An audience of one: Truman watches the dénouement 89

Figure 23. 'It's funny that you like the ballet, because I happen to have two tickets…' 89

Figure 24. 'You know if we'll get the overtime bonus on this one?' 89

Figure 25. Grainy Dana 90

Chapter 1: Into the Woods: Introduction

The Cabin in the Woods (2012), Drew Goddard's directorial debut, almost didn't make it out of the gate. Co-written in 2008 with Joss Whedon of *Buffy the Vampire Slayer* fame in a three-day marathon during which Goddard and Whedon sequestered themselves in a rented bungalow, the film was shot between March and May 2009 in Vancouver. Goddard and Whedon described their collaboration during both writing and filming as intimate and empathic, frequently referring to their 'hive mind' or their 'ids colliding,'[1] a sentiment echoed in some writings that have collapsed the two into a single entity named 'Whedard.'[2] Goddard and Whedon offered *Cabin* to studios as a take-it-or-leave-it package, 'in a move to lessen unnecessary meddling and keep the project as pure as possible.'[3] MGM won the bid for the film, but then shelved its February 2010 release in favour of the 3D makeover of *Avatar*. *Cabin*'s new release date of January 2011 was postponed again when MGM went bankrupt in November 2010.[4] The film was finally released in March 2012 after Lionsgate picked up the distribution rights. Shot on a relatively modest $30 million budget, at a time when 'the average [horror movie] budget had exploded to a massive $170 million,'[5] *Cabin* grossed $66.5 million worldwide—a box-office failure, given that a studio typically requires a worldwide gross of 2.5x budget to break even.[6] The film was nominated for 21 film association awards (with eight wins, one runner-up and one fifth place showing), including seven nominations (and two wins) for Best Screenplay, five nominations (and four wins) for Best Picture, and—strangely, given the intense hype in announcements and reviews—one nomination for best Overlooked Film of the Year (which *Cabin* didn't win).[7]

Early reviews agonised over the task of saying anything of substance without giving away the film's 'fun twist,'[8] which is that *Cabin* is simultaneously a bog-standard horror movie—'crushingly generic,' as one reviewer has it[9]—and a geeky meta-text twisting that story so far out of shape that some reviewers were left uncertain whether they had accidentally strayed into the wrong theatre.[10] While the theatrical release poster (fig. 1), with its Rubik's-cube cabin, heavily hints at the movie's 'twist,' the film's title and cabin plot-strand identify it as a generic exemplar. Five youngsters, three boys and two girls, disappear into a cabin in the woods to spend a weekend partying, two of them with explicit sexual plans (the kind for which you are always swiftly and messily dispatched in horror films). The five are promptly and predictably attacked by zombies. An hour later, the survivor count is down to two, a permanently stoned boy and Carol Clover's stereotypical 'Final Girl.'[11] These two discover what the audience has known from the start: that the entire story of their entrapment and deaths was environmentally and chemically engineered by a bunch of lab-coat clad bureaucrats in an underground facility, where they follow the victims' death struggles on their version of the Big Screen, drinking and eating, giggling and commenting, even betting on the manner of the youngsters' deaths. In one particularly repellent scene, the lab techs watch two of the doomed teenagers going off into the woods with unambiguous intentions (even these intentions are not entirely down to teen hormones but are manipulated by pheromones injected into the scenario from the lab), rooting for the girl to disrobe before the zombies get her.

Figure 1. Theatrical release poster for The Cabin in the Woods (2012)

What, if anything, could justify such despicable behaviour? The stated purpose of the slaughter is to 'appease the monsters': in the world of the scenario managers, every nightmare creature, from zombies to Dracula to Frankenstein's monster, is real. These monsters, while ghastly enough, pale beside the unspeakable horror of the 'Ancient Ones,' vengeful Gods slumbering 'below' and only kept at bay by an annual blood sacrifice, enacted in the form of a stereotypical horror flick (one per nation, with the USA and Japan boasting the cleanest kill records worldwide). When all other rituals, including the normally so dependable Japanese ritual, have failed and the world once again looks to America for salvation, the two survivors manage to break through from the lab-engineered woods to the lab itself. As they unleash the monsters on the technicians, the film turns into an unsurprising-yet-gratifying apocalyptic revenge-flick. At the end of the whole mess, the facility's Director informs her last two lab rats that the Ancient Ones will destroy the world unless the two sacrifice themselves willingly. And here is the viewer's conundrum: ethical hardwiring acquired in apocalypse movies compels us to believe that the human race must survive no matter what the cost, and that, to quote *The Wrath of Khan* (1982), 'the needs of the many outweigh the needs of the few.' But then we remember the lab techs making bets and rooting for a girl under death sentence to bare her tits, and the Director's ethical repackaging of slaughter as noble sacrifice begins to stick in our craw. The surviving teens, too, will have none of it. And so the Director's moral appeal goes down like a lead balloon, and the survivors decide that a world in which humans are capable of the deliberate slaughter of others, even in the 'cause' of species survival, is not worth saving. Apocalypse now, they say: 'Humanity… it's time to give someone else a chance.' The Director is dispatched by a teenaged zombie wielding a hatchet, and everyone else by a giant hand emerging from flaming depths, crushing the cabin, swatting at the viewer, and darkening the screen, thus enacting simultaneously the end of the film and the end of the world. Closing credits roll over the nerve-shredding strains of the Nine Inch Nails song 'Last' ('Pigs get what pigs deserve… This isn't meant to last').

The Cabin in the Woods has been the critics' marmite: either loved to bits or hated with a passion, very often for the same quality—its geeky self-referentiality.[12] There is virtually no neutral zone in reviews; one reviewer's 'clever' is another's 'too clever by half'; one critic's 'smart' is another's 'smartass.' Hailed variously as a 'reinvention' or 'correction' of the horror genre,[13] as 'a satire of the horror genre, a metaphor for the filming process, and a critique of society,'[14] as 'symbolically extending a middle finger to formulaic corporate horror and the sequels and remakes that have bogged the genre down in repetition,'[15] *Cabin* has by now developed a solid reputation as the horror genre's most allusive, intertextual and self-referential parody. Enthusiasts have, at best, credited the film with 'real greatness'[16] and at least mapped *Cabin* favourably against their notion of a stereotypical horror flick ('here's what *Cabin in the Woods* is not. It's not predictable. It's not stupid. And it's not a dreary exercise in torture porn').[17] Detractors have slammed the film for its 'off-putting vibe of cocky self-confidence, a "don't you get it" conviction that it's something special.'[18] Whether exultant or aggrieved, reviewers have overwhelmingly read *Cabin* as a meta-film, which many of them have taken to mean that it has already failed as a film. Reviewed purely for its concept (rather than its story, cinematography, characterisation, script, dialogue or visuals), the sole question that matters is whether *Cabin* is merely a geek-out for fanboys with nothing to offer that *Scream* (1996) had not already achieved[19] or a film that involves and implicates viewers in more serious ways. Positive reviews inevitably assume the latter, negative ones the former: 'you don't feel remorse or consternation after watching *The Cabin in the Woods*. It doesn't make you rethink your assumptions or ponder how you take pleasure. It lets you feel smart. Again.'[20] With the critical spotlight largely focusing on *Cabin* as a meta-text, the film engendered not only 'rabid fans but also snarling detractors' who delighted in giving the game away: 'this isn't just about disliking *The Cabin in the Woods*, it's about an almost primal need to spoil the movie.' Certainly, however, as this reviewer also points out, that visceral response—on both sides of the controversy—indicates that there is something more to see here: 'one of the hallmarks of a great film is that it truly divides people.'[21]

Similar divisions emerge from Joe Lipsett's study of *Cabin* reviews. At the time of his writing (2014), the film had been rated by 180,319 IMDb users. Lipsett's study of 100 of these reviews, 50 dating from the time of the film's theatrical release in the United States and 50 covering the time from 18 to 29 September 2012, divided reviewers into three groups: the *Competent/Satisfied*, *Competent/Disappointed* and the *Violator* group, who found their expectations of a horror film 'violated' and accordingly trashed the film, usually without references to content and without offering specific reasons. Lipsett found that in the other two groups, viewers who recognised *Cabin*'s use of self-reflexive and intertextual elements rated the film more highly than viewers less familiar with the horror genre and its history, and that while the intertextual allusions and jokes were one of the film's biggest draws for the *Competent/Satisfied* group, *Competent/Disappointed* viewers found this aspect far more polarising.[22]

For a film that has so often been dismissed as 'a minor success, a pleasant trifle,'[23] a 'climactic one-two punch of special-effects chaos and meta-movie chin stroking,'[24] *Cabin* has certainly provoked a great deal of scholarly thought. McNaughtan's bibliography on the film in the 2018 *Whedonverse Catalog* lists dozens of articles and books beneath his somewhat baffling comment that 'Study of *The Cabin in the Woods* is still in its infancy.'[25] The film has been—to cite just a small sample of the wealth of ideas it inspired—convincingly interpreted as an expression of generational conflict[26] and of America's globalisation fears;[27] as a critique of the myth of American exceptionalism[28] and as an attack on austerity;[29] as an anti-horror movie[30] and as a visualisation of Thacker's thought experiment of the '*world-without-us*';[31] as a tentatively feminist work[32] and as a film that objectifies women all over again;[33] as a Utopian film[34] and as a 'bleak and bitter work'[35] that emanates, to cite one of the most recent analysts of the film, 'from an idea that the system itself is evil.'[36] As is the case in reviews, the film has also attracted its fair share of scholarly work focusing on its inter- and metatextuality,[37] and justifiably so, since *Cabin* unquestionably and gleefully plays with, hints at, experiments with, twists, turns and upends great precursor texts. That may be the film's biggest draw,[38] but it is not, as I will argue further on, what has made the film sufficiently significant to inspire hundreds of thousands of reviews and, at this point, a burgeoning body of intelligent research. The fun in film-spotting, the raptures of recognition, the smugness of superiority, the eager acceptance of the film's invitation to 'feel smart. Again,' are merely the stones on which viewers hop, skip and jump across the river. They are the means, not the end; part of the journey, not the destination. Before we get there, though, it is worth turning over some of these stones.

The number of horror films referenced briefly in *Cabin* is staggering. Monsters from no fewer than 56 different films—unicorns, ghosts, mermen, dragons, a ballerina dentata, doll mask killers, witches, wraiths, giant snakes, the 'wet girl' typical of Japanese horror, Fornicus, Lord of Bondage and Pain (a figure reminiscent of *Hellraiser*'s Hell Lord), Romero's zombies, *The Evil Dead*'s 'Angry Molesting Tree,' the clown from *It*, the twins from *The Shining* and many more—make a cameo appearance,[39] and cataloguing these monsters has become somewhat of a spectator sport amongst *Cabin* aficionados.⁴⁰ Amid these rich pickings, six precursors—by no means an exhaustive list⁴¹—deserve a closer look because they are more central either to *Cabin*'s surface story (the cabin-plot, set literally and metaphorically on the surface) or to its meta-text, the story played out in the subterranean facility. The surface story draws on Tobe Hooper's *The Texas Chain Saw Massacre* (1974), Sam Raimi's *The Evil Dead* (1981)⁴² and Eli Roth's *Cabin Fever* (2002); its myth and meta-text on H. P. Lovecraft's short story 'The Call of Cthulhu' (1928), Wes Craven's *Scream* (1996), and Michael Haneke's *Funny Games* (1997/2007).

Cabin-movies are the ideal launch pad for self-aware and intertextual horror. 'Why does it *have* to be "The Cabin in the Woods?"' asks Murphy in her broad study of the rural American Gothic, and answers her own question: 'because this is the true starting point of American horror. […] The cabin in the woods is to the American Gothic what the haunted castle is to the European—the seed from which everything else ultimately grows.'⁴³ Likewise, Clover's 'Terrible Place,' the home of horror, is rural: 'An enormous proportion of horror takes as its starting point the visit or move of (sub)urban people to the country […]. Going from city to country in the horror film is […] like going from village to the deep, dark forest in the traditional fairy tale. […] The point is that rural Connecticut (or wherever), like the deep forests of Central Europe, is a place where the rules of civilisation do not obtain.'⁴⁴ Danger always lurks in the woods, and at the heart of horror is the suspicion that the savage will always overwhelm the civilised if given half a chance. Variations amount to differences of degree that leave this basic blueprint intact. Murphy's taxonomy of horror, for example, focuses on the question how—not whether—civilisation will be crushed. In Type A of rural Gothic narrative, those who leave civilisation become less civilised themselves (Peckinpah's *Straw Dogs* (1971); Kubrick's *The Shining* (1980); Myrick and Sánchez's *The Blair Witch Project* (1999); Holland and Mitton's *YellowBrickRoad* (2010));⁴⁵ in Type B, the civilised who venture into the wild remain distinct from but become the target of barbarians, showing that too much time in the boonies renders people savage to the point of unrecognisability (as in *The Texas Chain Saw Massacre*; Craven's *The Hills Have Eyes* (1977); Kiersch's *Children of the Corn* (1984), and every cabin-movie ever made).⁴⁶ Such niceties aside, the basic premise of cabin-films is part of America's cultural stream-of-subconsciousness, instantly gettable and familiar 'not merely because cabins are prevalent in so many horror movies, but because the cabin scenarios inherently describe the ambiguous relationship modern humans have with wilderness.'[47] Even an audience ignorant of horror traditions 'doesn't need to have it explained to them [...]: they've seen it all before.'[48]

Precursor-films like *The Texas Chain Saw Massacre*, *The Evil Dead* and *Cabin Fever*[49] (the latter both precursor and a meta-text in its own right) already assume a considerable degree of audience familiarity with the horror blueprint: the clash between the wild and the civilised; the cabin and surrounding woods as the site of slaughter; the no-way-back notion (the road that leads from civilisation to the wilderness is a one-way-street), and the victim-blaming that precludes audience identification. In all cases, five teens (three girls and two guys in Raimi's film, three guys and two girls in the other two) set out to the country for a weekend of fun and games. *Texas Chain Saw* and *Cabin Fever* feature the obligatory gas station scene, where they receive (and naturally ignore) an oblique warning that they're about to drive into disaster (in *Evil Dead*, that function is served by a near-fatal accident on the way to the cabin). All three films engage in the victim-blaming typical of classic horror by characterising the sacrificial lambs mostly by their stupid decisions, encouraging a 'would you really...?'-smugness in the audience that permits revelling in the slaughter unimpeded by sympathy or identification. Visiting slaughterhouses for fun (*Texas Chain Saw*); playing around with weird artefacts, often made of animal or human remains (*Texas Chain Saw*; *Evil Dead*); traipsing through the woods at night, either while pushing a guy in a wheelchair (*Texas Chain Saw*) or, more frequently, because 'I know someone's out there...' (*Evil Dead*); and reading incantations in ancient languages that raise the dead (*Evil Dead*) are all par for the course.

While the doomed teens of these films are guilty of no more than bad decision-making and an unhealthy disrespect for the unknown—hardly sins that, in a normal ethical universe, merit the death penalty—Roth's *Cabin Fever*, which, like *The Cabin in the Woods* already builds on many of these conventional tropes, considerably exacerbates both the teens' idiocy and their culpability. Transgressions comprise immediate and casual sex (Jeff and Marcy; Paul and Karen); lewd campfire stories involving sex toys, masturbation and dogs licking one's balls (communal sin); setting a fire in the woods and walking away (Bert); exulting in one's sole survivor-status in heartless disregard for everyone else's death (Jeff); accidentally shooting a plague victim and leaving him without reporting the incident (Bert again); and burning the same victim when he comes to the cabin pleading for help and then leaving him for dead in the woods (communal sin). Roth's film also links these sins more directly with their punishment: the plague victim they first shoot and then burn to near-death manages to stumble into the town's reservoir where he expires, thus spreading the plague to all who drink the water. The youngsters are thus essentially cast as the authors of their own demise. Notably, too, the disease seems specifically designed to punish their debauchery: attacking primarily innards and privates, the plague proves the ultimate killjoy for the oversexed teens.

In all three films, the border between the wilderness and civilisation is both invisible and inflexible. Once you cross, there is no way back. Usually, this crossover point is represented by the gas station; in *The Evil Dead*, the concept is more concretely represented by a wooden bridge that falls apart after the teens cross it (a low-tech ancestor of the collapsing mountain tunnel and invisible barrier in *The Cabin in the Woods*). The message, in all three, is clear: 'hillbillies' and 'civilised' people don't mix, and if civilisation stumbles into the wilderness, civilisation will be wiped out, leaving the wilderness untouched. This, too, is a trope that *Cabin Fever*, in its capacity as a borderline meta-horrorflick, playfully adapts. In Roth's film, it is the 'civilised' teens— not, as is customary, the indigenous 'savages'—who are the authors of their own destruction. They are deemed to deserve it not, as per usual, through mere stupidity and minor transgressions like drinking or having sex, but by virtue of extreme and escalating heartlessness and criminality (first refusing to aid the sick man; then shooting him; and, finally, killing him). What is more, the wilderness is by no means as backwards as it appears. The point is made in the initial harbinger scene at the gas station, where the general store owner, when asked what the huge rifle on the wall is for, answers: 'That's for niggers.' The teens turn away in amused disgust, undoubtedly eliciting a mirroring response from most viewers. Post-slaughter, the film's final scene returns us to the gas station and general store, where three Black people pick up that same rifle, which they had left with the store owner to be cleaned and polished. The greeting between owner and customers is Harlem-style cool and raucously jovial: 'Hi, my nigga, how are you?—What's up, nigga?—Where you been, man?' accompanied by homie handshakes. Is this a bit of breezy social Utopianism advocating the merger of seemingly incompatible cultures, and never mind all the liberal agonising about cultural appropriation and offensive language? The film's final scene seems to offer another hint in that direction: closing credits roll to the sound of a bluegrass band playing on the store front, with those peeking past the credits treated to the sight of three big city 'niggas' (the store owner's moniker for Black people) happily dancing in place behind the 'hillbilly' band.

For the most part, *Cabin*'s most direct ancestors adhere to the formula of cabin-horror that pits a frail civilisation against an impervious wilderness. In *The Evil Dead* and *Cabin Fever*, the rout of the teens is total, with only *Texas Chain Saw* featuring a stereotypical Final Girl. Unmoved by these events, the wilderness returns to its normal savage self in *Evil Dead* and *Texas Chain Saw*. *Cabin Fever*, on the other hand, again deviates from formula by wiping out the wild and the civilised, country and city alike. The final shot, again partially hidden behind rolling credits, focuses briefly on local cops buying 5-cent lemonade made with diseased water, then on a delivery truck labelled 'Down Home Spring Water' as it pulls out of the gas station, on its way to exporting the plague to towns and cities across America.

Cabin's plot heavily leans on the narrative structure of these films. It copies their visuals—Goddard's cabin and surrounding woods (fig. 2) bear distinct similarities to Raimi's (fig. 3) and Roth's (fig. 4)—and cheerfully rips off plot devices: *Evil Dead*'s self-opening cellar trap door and collapsing bridge, its evil book and zombie-raising incantation all play a starring role in Goddard's film.[50] No less evident are *Cabin*'s debts on the metatextual and mythological level. From Lovecraft's literature, the film inherited its 'Ancient Ones' who end up destroying the world after the ritual fails.[51] To Lovecraft, these evil Gods are not mere monsters but part of a larger teleology of humanity, which he saw 'not as the focus, product or creation of the divine, but rather as utterly incidental to it: fire and brimstone without the chance of personal salvation.'[52] Almost all of Lovecraft's published work is haunted by the 'Great Old Ones,' ancient, evil deities who once ruled the Earth and have since fallen into a deep sleep, leaving humans in blessed ignorance of their existence. The Old Ones form part of a purposeless, mechanical and uncaring universe which the blessedly puny faculties of humans are unable to fathom, and of which the merest glimpse would drive them instantly insane. 'The Call of Cthulhu,' the first of Lovecraft's tales to expand on the theme, briefly sketches the Gods' history on Planet Earth:

Those Old Ones were gone now, inside the earth and under the sea; but their dead bodies had told their secrets in dreams to the first men, who formed a cult which had never died. [...] These Great Old Ones [...] were not composed altogether of flesh and blood. [...] But although They no longer lived, They would never really die. They all lay in stone houses [...], preserved by the spells of mighty Cthulhu for a glorious resurrection when the stars and the earth might once more be ready for Them. But at that time some force from outside must serve to liberate Their bodies.[53]

That time, in Lovecraft's tales, is always nigh. The evil Gods' 'ministers on Earth still bellow and prance and slay around idol-capped monoliths in lonely places,' always ready to raise the Old Ones through human sacrifice and transform the world into a place 'screaming with fright and frenzy.' This is the poisonous crop from which *Cabin* harvested not only its Ancient Ones but also their 'ministers' (the Director and employees of the underground facility) and the method (human sacrifice), with a slight plot twist: in Lovecraft's texts, human sacrifice heralds and prepares the evil Gods' return; in *Cabin*, it is offered to *prevent* it, 'in humility and fear, for the blessed peace of your eternal slumber.'

Figures 2–4. Look-alike cabins (clockwise from top L) in The Cabin in the Woods, The Evil Dead *and* Cabin Fever

Other films prefigure both *Cabin*'s self-referentiality and its implication of the audience. Wes Craven's *Scream* (1996) made near-constant self-referential jokes an instant classic feature of spoof horror. Virtually every conversation in the film is drenched in movie references, the point being that the film's high school students have seen so many films that they've lost all ability to distinguish between the movies and real life. There is no reality beyond that displayed on a screen, and screen culture—most often horror culture—provides every anchor and reference point for their lives. Seduction and sex is framed as a move from 'edited for television' to a 'nice solid R-rating on our way to an NC-17'; the film's killer plays a game with his victims where he forces them to guess the names of killers in famous horror flicks before he guts them. In one of the film's now most famous scenes, horror geek Randy (Jamie Kennedy) lists the three most basic survival rules of horror: never have sex (because only virgins can survive a horror film); never drink or do drugs, and 'Never, ever, under any circumstances, say: "I'll be right back." 'Cause you won't be back.' All theories about the killer and the crime are informed not by the real but the reel world, from *Basic Instinct* (1992) to *Ricki Lake* (1993–2004). Feelings of terror, too, are described in movie terms: at one point, the film's main heroine is informed by a friend that she's acting like a chick in 'a Wes Carpenter flick' (a whimsical amalgamation of John Carpenter, one of horror's icons, and *Scream*'s own director Wes Craven). There is more than a hint here that teens are desensitised by screen violence, expressed, for instance, in their nonchalant discussion of the gruesome murder of classmates: 'we're not just talking killed, we're talking splatter-movie killed. Ripped open from end to end.' In one particularly obnoxious scene, a number of drunk youngsters, upon hearing that their school principal was 'gutted and hung from the goalpost on the football field,' race off to the scene, cheering and whooping, to get a good look before he's taken down, as if there was nothing more hilarious than seeing your teacher with his guts hanging out. To traditionalists, the message is clear: these kids are completely inured to extra-diegetic life, and the movies, particularly horror movies, are to blame.

To launch its half-hearted critique[54] of screen violence and its effects on the young, *Scream* feels obliged to at least attempt to draw the line between horror movie culture and real life. The only teen who seems to understand the difference is Sidney Prescott (Neve Campbell), the film's previously traumatised victim (by the rape and murder of her mother a year before the film's action begins) and now the killer's main target. She is the only character in the film who expresses a dislike of horror films. 'What's the point?' she asks the killer on the phone. 'They're all the same. Some stupid killer stalking some big-breasted girl who can't act who's always running up the stairs when she should be going out the front door. It's insulting.' She is also the only character who sporadically attempts to break out of movie-land. Having refused her boyfriend Billy (Skeet Ulrich) sex for two years, she finally relents, explaining to him her fear of turning out like her sexually licentious mother, 'like *The Bad Seed*, or something.' This makes sense to Billy: 'It's like Jodie Foster in *The Silence of the Lambs*, when she keeps having flashbacks of her dead father.' When Sidney tries to steer him back to reality—'But this is life. This isn't a movie'—he counters: 'Sure it is, Sid. It's all—it's all a movie. It's all one great big movie. Only you can't pick your genre.' What Billy is indicating here is that while she, finally consenting to sex, may think she is in a romantic comedy, she is really the heroine in a horror flick, eligible for slaughter after committing the horror film's cardinal sin and losing her virginity. Sure enough, Billy, the boy who deflowers her, also turns out to be one of the film's two killers. In her confrontation with the pair, who have launched the killing spree in homage to horror movie killers and are already planning 'a sequel,' Sidney once again tries to inject some reality into the scenario: 'You sick fucks,' she tells them. 'You've seen one too many movies.' But in the end, she falls back into the reel world in which she, too, spends much of her mental life. Looking down at Billy's corpse, horror fan Randy, another survivor (due to his own virginity, he surmises) warns Sidney: 'Careful. This is the moment when the supposedly dead killer comes back to life for one last scare.' Billy gasps on cue, lunging for them, upon which Sidney shoots him in the head with the words, 'Not in my movie.'

The film's critique of desensitisation through horror movie violence rests squarely on the distinction between everyone else's movie and Sidney's reality—her grief and trauma after losing her mother to a horrific murder; her incapacity for intimacy due to post-traumatic stress; her helplessness and terror at finding herself the target of her mother's killer. But Sidney's real world is profoundly undermined by the fact that she moves equally willingly and fluently in the reel world everyone else inhabits. Like everyone else's, her real-life experience can only be expressed by weak similes ripped from the movies. Her hometown, turned into a ghost town by the police curfew, reminds her of *The Town that Dreaded Sundown* (1976), just like her fear that she might have inherited her mother's sexual proclivities instantly calls to mind Mervyn LeRoy's film *The Bad Seed* (1956). Her tragedy, strangled by the film's far more prominent comedy, never achieves escape velocity, which throws the film's self-referentiality back onto itself without implicating the audience in any meaningful way. Viewers more amused by inside jokes than moved by Sidney's pain are unlikely to perceive themselves as an ethically incriminated horror movie audience relishing the slaughter. Rather, *Scream*'s teens provide viewers simultaneously with a diegetic and an extra-diegetic model of anti/identification. On the one hand, the audience can geek out with them, delighting in the deciphering of subtle inferences and heavy hints; on the other, it is invited to feel superior to them, the puerile near-psychopaths who have no points of reference, no imagination, no ethical anchor and no powers of articulation beyond those spoon-fed to them by screen culture.

A year after *Scream* failed to make the horror audience aware of its own guilty involvement, Michael Haneke attempted to make the point again in *Funny Games* (originally Austria 1997; remade in 2007 for an American audience).[55] Haneke's film tells the harrowing tale of a home invasion where two white-gloved serial killers who call themselves 'Peter' and 'Paul' murder a family of three (husband, wife and a little boy) at their vacation home after gruesome physical and emotional torture.[56] At the end it emerges that they tour vacation homes around the lake, killing families at random and for no fathomable reason.

Signs of *Cabin*'s indebtedness to Haneke's work include both minor and fairly significant aspects. The minor ones are the distinct visual and aural similarity of the films' opening and closing sequences. Both feature tall block lettering in blood red (in the opening sequence of both versions of Haneke's film as well as the opening sequence of Goddard's).[57] Both choose a highly discordant metal/grindcore track for a credit sequence, the Nine Inch Nails song 'Last' over Goddard's closing credits and the Naked City tracks 'Bonehead' and 'Hellraiser' over Haneke's opening credits (in both versions). 'Bonehead' and 'Hellraiser' are both 'hardcore miniatures,' coming in at under a minute each and featuring inarticulate screams and howls over heavy discordant electric guitar chords, but no actual lyrics. The soundtrack is meant to jar with the cheerfully relaxed and loving interaction of the family in the car, drowning out the soothing Handel aria, 'Care selve, ombre beate,' they have chosen for the trip. Before the film has even properly begun, the Naked City tracks, described by one reviewer as sounding 'like an orgy that turned into a massacre,'[58] announce to the audience that the family is already well on its way there.

More significant than these aesthetic and allusive parallels, though, are the ways in which Haneke forces viewer identification with the killers (rather than with the victims, as ethics would seem to dictate). Several times throughout the brutalisation of the family, one of the killers breaks the fourth wall, looking straight at the camera (the audience) and winking; asking viewers whether they've had enough yet, even—in one case—rewinding and restarting a scene. Peter and Paul bet with their victims that the entire family will be dead in twelve hours, upon which Paul turns to the audience and smirks: 'What do you think? Do you think they have a chance to win? You are on their side, aren't you? So, where do you place your bets?' The film's ghastly 'funny games' always involve the doomed family, as in the scene in which the family is made to search for their dog's corpse, with the killer giving the family hot, warm and cold clues. The game is torture, the purpose of dragging it out before the kill is entertainment: 'We do want to offer something to the audience,' says Paul ('wir wollen doch dem Publikum etwas bieten'). *Funny Games*, in other words, impeaches the horror viewer for being entertained by watching a family ripped to pieces. We, the audience are not, as Paul says with a sarcastic wink, 'on their side,' not even innocent bystanders, but rather—so long as we continue to watch—accomplices after the fact.

Haneke's films are fairly explicit in their attempt to elicit this insight from audiences. In various interviews, he has claimed both that his films 'rape' his viewers to force them 'to become autonomous'[59] and that an ideal audience response to his films would be if viewers, unable to withstand the images he shows them, simply looked away.[60] Haneke (and *Cabin*, in launching a similar challenge 10 to 15 years later) ran a considerable risk by positing the guilty involvement of the audience: nobody likes to be guilt-tripped. How much audiences dislike it emerges clearly from reviews of *Funny Games*. Frank Kermode saw it in Cannes and resented 'being told off for two hours. By an Austrian. In France.'[61] Daniela Sannwald has savaged Haneke in—of all places—her foreword to an issue of a film magazine dedicated to Haneke's work, where she labels him a 'monomaniacal moralist' out to ensnare his audience: 'The joke is that [Haneke turns] the viewer into the killer's accomplice and then ultimately [reproaches] him with that very thing. It is a perfidious method to bring home to the viewer what he really is: a voyeur.'[62] Even the accusation of latent fascism and authoritarianism, the worst indictment imaginable for any German or Austrian, has been lobbed at Haneke in response to *Funny Games*:

> Symptomatic of the fascist mind-set is the self-righteous application of a strict code of civility from which the ruler himself is naturally exempt. Thus, Haneke despises the mass audience's vicarious pleasure in make-believe mayhem while demonstrating his own capacity to dish it out. The most honest aspect of Haneke's movies is the evident satisfaction the director derives from the authoritarian aspects of his position—demonstrated most spectacularly in *Funny Games* when the worm, as it were, finally turns. The wheel is rigged so that only Haneke can win.[63]

Clearly, *Funny Games* struck a nerve. Much like later critics of *The Cabin in the Woods*, reviewers tend to focus on the film's purported intention while ignoring the film itself. This may be a stance that particularly plagues films by directors commonly considered 'auteurs,' like Haneke: auteur-films are perceived as authorial 'statements' and judged on the quality of that statement alone. (Interestingly enough, critics who view *The Cabin in the Woods* as an auteur-film inevitably regard it as Whedon's work, not Goddard's: in reviews and scholarship, there is such a thing as the 'Whedonverse,' even the 'Cabin-verse,' but never a Goddard-verse.)[64] Reviews in pursuit of *Cabin*'s 'statement' at times subordinate discussion of narrative, cinematography, dialogue or visuals to aspects completely incidental to the film, not unlike the 'passport control' reviews bringing up Haneke's nationality or linking his work vicariously to his home country's bygone fascist regime. In this respect, as well, *Funny Games* is an unwitting precursor to *The Cabin in the Woods*: the critical reception of both raises the question of how an audience will react when a film dares to point out their own guilty involvement.[65]

Less imperiously than *Funny Games* but no less efficiently,[66] this is, in fact, precisely what Goddard's film does. In what follows, I would like to make the argument that *Cabin* can, as many have already said, be considered a reinvention, parody and correction of the horror tradition, but for reasons different from the ones usually offered. These reasons are rooted not merely in clever quotes and hints at genre conventions, but in philosophical points that target both horror and its audience. *The Cabin in the Woods* is not only a meta-text and commentary on the genre, but also its belated prototype.

It took a film like *Cabin* to point out that horror films regularly raise ethical questions implicating the viewer, and that horror itself possesses aesthetic and philosophical capacities that are habitually underrated (often by critics surmising, like those citing Haneke's 'fascist mind-set,' that the genre has the wrong 'pedigree').[67] Yet despite the film's clear focus on ethics, despite the common acknowledgement that 'Whedon's corpus is commendably philosophical in nature,'[68] and despite the fact that *Cabin*'s meta-horror status would clearly suggest such a reading, philosophical interpretations of the film are rare. Of the two works that have taken a philosophical approach, Jared Richardson's MA thesis (2015) offers an insightful reading of nihilism in the film in the context of Thacker's *Horror of Philosophy*, while Dean A. Kowalski's essay in *Joss Whedon as Philosopher* reduces *Cabin*'s philosophical potential to a shallow morality play on the benefits and dangers of the horror genre.[69] *Cabin*'s 'philosophy' according to Kowalski amounts to no more than the bald statement that 'bad' horror movies desensitise viewers to violence whereas 'good' ones 'can beneficially serve as an inoculation against real fear.'[70] Goddard's film (in Kowalski's reading Whedon's film) thus encourages the audience to either 'cease exposing ourselves to it, even if in some sense it is titillating to watch such movies,' or else to 'gravitate towards aesthetically valuable horror films and away from those that offer us poor inoculations.'[71]

There is, then, a real void when it comes to reading what is so obviously a philosophical film (Kowalski is right about that much, at least) in a philosophical context. In the following four chapters, I will stake a small claim in this rich and thus far largely unexplored field. The first two sections, which we might call the 'diegetic' chapters, will focus on philosophical points made in the film itself: the struggle between faith and nihilism, the ethical implications of (self-)sacrifice, the place of humanity in the world, and the question of free will. The final two chapters will consider extra-diegetic aspects, principally the question of how *Cabin*, itself a philosophical text, elicits a philosophical response from the viewer. This topic will be explored with the help of two sub-disciplines of philosophy, aesthetics (which asks how audiences see) and ethics (which asks why they look).

Critics have tended to read Joss Whedon's now famous description of *Cabin* as his 'loving hate-letter to horror'[72] as exclusively critical, a remark that decries the genre's clichés, its banality, its contempt for the audience, or its descent into torture porn.[73]

Few have bothered to ask what there is to love about horror. Yet clearly, Whedon's formulation points not only at the genre's shortcomings but also at its possibilities. With regard to *Cabin* itself, critics have sometimes suffered from the same blind spot, accepting it as an allusive meta-text ('It lets you feel smart. Again') but denying its more profound effect on the viewer: 'It doesn't make you rethink your assumptions or ponder how you take pleasure.'[74] This, as I hope to show, is a severe underestimation of *The Cabin in the Woods*, and even more so of the genre the film quotes and parodies, epitomises and celebrates, loves and hates.

Notes

1. The process is lovingly described in several interviews; see, among many others, interviews with Goddard and Whedon for the DVD supplementary feature, 'We Are Not Who We Are'; Lavery 151–2; Metz para. 1. On the making of the film, see also McNaughtan 215 and Pascale 319, 321 and 323–4.
2. For instance Sterba: 'It is impossible to tease the Goddard out of the "Whed-dard" film *The Cabin in the Woods*' (146); further on in the same essay she settles on the moniker 'Whedard' accompanied by a singular verb (162).
3. See Taylor's *IndieWire* interview with Drew Goddard.
4. See Conaton 101, 440; Giannini, 'Belly' 88.
5. 'Horror Movie Budgets.'
6. On *Cabin*'s box office performance, see Hammond 34 and Nelson para. 13.
7. Awards are listed on the film's Wikipedia site.
8. See, for example, the review by Neumaier in the *New York Daily News*.
9. See the review by J. R. Jones in the *Chicago Reader*.
10. 'Are we in the right theater? That was the first fleeting thought that went through my head during the opening few seconds of Drew Goddard's *Cabin in the Woods*' (Buckwalter).
11. The 'Final Girl,' a term originally coined by Carol Clover in *Men, Women and Chain Saws*, has since become one of the most recognised tropes of the horror genre (sufficiently established to merit its own Wikipedia entry; see 'Final Girl') and a major theme in feminist horror criticism. The term describes the sole survivor, nearly always female, of the massacre enacted in the film. She survives the slaughter of her companions to face the killer alone, (often) escapes altogether and (sometimes) tells the story of the slaughter. In Clover's

analysis, the Final Girl raises interesting questions about the depiction of women in horror and slasher films, the ability of a predominantly male audience to identify with a female character and the genre's relationship with feminism. Famous Final Girls include Laurie Strode in John Carpenter's *Halloween* (1978), Sally in Tobe Hooper's *The Texas Chainsaw Massacre* (1974), and Ellen Ripley in the *Alien* franchise.

12. Obviously, critical reviews may (try to) steer audience responses, with various degrees of success, but one should not be confused with the other (compare the critic's take with, for example, Joe Lipsett's snapshot of audience reviews in his analysis of IMDB reviews). I would surmise that most readers' responses to critical reviews, perhaps much like most viewers' responses to films, fall into the 'negotiating' category (as opposed to 'dominant' or 'oppositional'; see Stuart Hall's audience positioning theory). Interestingly, the divided response in critical reviews to *Cabin*'s self-referential 'cleverness' holds true both for those published in the mainstream press and for those in more genre-specific publications like *Fangoria* or *Dread Central*.

13. Graves (unpag.).

14. Mayo 236, quoting Goddard and Whedon.

15. Kooyman 115.

16. Review by Katey Rich in *Cinema Blend*; see also Joe Morgenstern's review of the film as 'borderline-brilliant' in the *Wall Street Journal*.

17. Review by Lewis Wallace in *Wired*; see also Eric Goldman's view of the film as 'an incredibly clever and fun take on classic horror movie' ('*The Cabin in the Woods*: What's Truly Lurking in the Darkness') and Michael Gingold's highly enthusiastic review in *Fangoria*.

18. Review by Mark Olsen in *Village Voice*; similarly in the following reviews: A. O. Scott in *The New York Times* ('There is a scholarly, nerdy, completist sensibility at work here that is impressive until it becomes exhausting'); Dana Stevens in *Slate* ('If Goddard and Whedon's smart-aleck goof is all it takes to change the slasher-movie game, that may just prove it's a game that really needed changing'); David Rooney in *Hollywood Reporter* ('when the meta-references take over at the expense of character or plot, the knowing self-amusement wears thin'); Becca James in *AV Club* ('It's not winking; it's assaulting'; see McLevy and James); and Kim Newman in her overall positive review in *Sight & Sound* ('too clever by half').

19. Ali Caterall's review, for example, pours cold water on the idea that *Cabin* '"turns the genre inside out." Well, yes, I suppose it does. But only in some remote parallel universe where *Scream*, *My Little Eye* and *Scooby-Doo* didn't already exist. […] Essentially, it's an overlong, pumped-up *Twilight Zone* episode.' See also the review of the film script in *Scriptshadow*: '*Cabin In The Woods* would like to *think* that it's making you think, but all they're doing is trying to create the next Scream.'

20. Review by Cynthia Fuchs in *PopMatters*.
21. Review by Devin Faraci in *Badass Digest*.
22. Lipsett paras 17, 29–30.
23. Review by Dana Stevens in *Slate*.
24. Review by J. R. Jones in the *Chicago Reader*.
25. McNaughtan 215.
26. Renner.
27. Wagner.
28. Cooper.
29. Mayo.
30. McDonald.
31. Richardson.
32. Vineyard.
33. Sessarego.
34. Derrick King.
35. Woofter and Stokes.
36. The citation is taken from Kendall R. Phillips's talk 'A Certain Tendency in Post-Occupy Cinema'; in the eponymous book chapter, *Cabin* is one of his three case studies embodying the post-occupy 'affect of feeling' that identifies the 'system' itself as 'evil.'
37. For example, in Giannini, 'Charybdis'; Hammond; McDonald; Metz; Venezia; and Canavan, 'Nightmares.'
38. See the comments on the pleasures of intertextuality as an affirmation of audience 'expertise' offered by Moldenhauer (in 'Pigs' 29) and Richardson 28.
39. See the list of films offered on the IMDb webpage 'Horror Films Referenced in The Cabin in the Woods.'
40. Nelson para. 28: 'The entire sequence [...] almost challenges the horror fan to identify the various monsters [...]. And horror fans, aided by high-definition Blu-Ray screen captures, have been more than up to the challenge. A simple Internet search for "Cabin in the Woods monsters" leads to hundreds of posts and pages dedicated to the topic. From the IMDb to wikis and message boards to film and pop culture websites, cataloguing the monsters seems to be by far the number one online preoccupation of horror fans when it comes to *The Cabin in the Woods*.' A search with the search terms suggested by Nelson on 18 April 2020 netted me 4,530,000 results in 0.53 seconds. On *Cabin*'s 'stable of monsters,' see

also Kooyman 113; Starr para. 3; Mayo 244–5; Metz para. 8; Richardson 53; and Graves, who found the following items on TVTropes.org, a collection of user-inventoried content: "'The Abandoned Cabin,' "Ancient Evil," the "Creepy Basement," "Creepy Children," "Dangerous Widows," "Death by Sex," "Dropping the Weapon," "Dumb Blondes," "Dumb Jocks," a "Final Girl," the "Jump Scare," "Let's Split Up, Gang," an "Ominous Music Box Tune," "Summoning Artifacts," a "Surprisingly Sudden Death," "Taxidermy Terror," and the "Torture Cellar."'

41. Other films that could have played in the 'significant precursor' league (but were benched for reasons of space) include Sean S. Cunningham's *Friday the 13th* (1980), George Romero's *Night of the Living Dead* (1968), John Carpenter's *The Thing* (1982) and *Big Trouble in Little China* (1986), Stanley Kubrick's *Dr. Strangelove* (1964), George Roy Hill's *Butch Cassidy and the Sundance Kid* (1969), Charles T. Barton's *Abbott and Costello Meet Frankenstein* (1948), and, of course, Ridley Scott's *Alien* (1979). Drew Goddard listed *The Thing*, *Dr. Strangelove*, *Big Trouble* and *Butch* as direct influences on his film (Wright). Further precursor films are suggested by Weyant para. 10.

42. On the film's indebtedness to Raimi's work, see Graves, and Weyant para. 8.

43. Murphy 15.

44. Clover 124; see also Weyant para. 6 on the 'Terrible Place.'

45. '[T]he universal realization of cabin scenarios is that, ironically, one must become wild in order to survive the wilderness long enough to return to civilization' (Weyant para. 14).

46. Murphy 10–13.

47. Weyant para. 2.

48. Murphy 15.

49. On links between *Cabin* and Hooper's and Raimi's films, see Hammond; Nelson (para. 15) has pointed to *Cabin*'s indebtedness to all three.

50. See particularly Lockett 131, and Graves on the links between Goddard's and Raimi's films, which to her include not merely allusive items and plot devices, but also lighting and framing.

51. On the film's debts to Lovecraft's tales, see, among others, Blouin, 'Growing Global Darkness' 91; Lavery 151; Lockett 127; Poole 214–5. Poole makes it clear that the reference to Lovecraft's evil Gods was a deliberate decision on the part of Goddard and Whedon (215).

52. Lockett 128.

53. This and all further quotations from the text in Lovecraft, 'The Call of Cthulhu' (unpag.).

54. 'Half-hearted' for obvious reasons: Wes Craven, the film's director, and Kevin Williamson, who authored the screenplay, are both masters at disseminating the desensitising violence

they're critiquing in *Scream*, having had long and successful careers in the production of horror and slasher films.

55. My remarks in what follows will refer to aspects common to both and differentiate where necessary.
56. See Wurmitzer's work for a good interpretation of the film.
57. Pointed out by Venezia 413.
58. The G-Wing, comment on the YouTube version of Haneke's opening sequence (US version).
59. Interview with Stefan Grissemann and Michael Omasta: 'sie vergewaltigt den Zuschauer zur Selbständigkeit' (205).
60. Haneke's remark is cited in Krenn 89.
61. Cited in McCann and Sorfa 3.
62. My translation of 'Man hat es bei Haneke mit einem monomanischen Moralisten zu tun [...]. Der Witz dabei ist, dass ich den Zuschauer zum Komplizen des Täters mache und ihm genau das am Schluss vorwerfe. Das ist eine heimtückische Methode, um ihm vor Augen zu führen, was er eigentlich ist, nämlich ein Voyeur' (Sannwald 3–4).
63. Hoberman in a 1998 review of *Funny Games* in *The Village Voice*, cited in Wheatley 28.
64. Joe Lipsett points this out repeatedly in his study of hundreds of reviews: 'a number of Competent/Satisfied reviewers identified themselves as Joss Whedon fans [...]. Interestingly, in the majority of these cases, director Drew Goddard is overlooked or given brief mention [...]. In general there are significantly fewer references to Goddard and none mention Goddard without also mentioning Whedon' (paras 31–2; note 9).
65. For an insightful analysis of *Funny Games* and *The Cabin in the Woods* as vicarious experiences of violence and the interpellation of their own viewers, see Venezia 413–14.
66. Moldenhauer and Richardson have both pointed to the difference in tone between Haneke's and *Cabin*'s genre-critique (Moldenhauer, 'Pigs' 18 and Richardson, citing Tasha Robinson, 8).
67. 'The horror film has long been one of the most routinely maligned of genres. Horror scholars have noted—some with relish, others with regret—its clichéd status as "the most disreputable of Hollywood genres"' (Kooyman 102).
68. Kowalski, *Joss Whedon as Philosopher* 2.
69. Kowalski, *Joss Whedon as Philosopher*; see also his and S. Evan Kreider's 'Introduction' to *The Philosophy of Joss Whedon*.
70. Kowalski, *Joss Whedon as Philosopher* 192.
71. Kowalski, *Joss Whedon as Philosopher* 197.

72. See his interview with Andrew Patrick Nelson, para. 9; McNaughtan 215; Canavan, 'Nightmares' paras 7 and 16.
73. Summed up by McNaughtan 215.
74. Review by Cynthia Fuchs in *PopMatters*.

Chapter 2: Fealty v. Nihilism: How (Not) to Save the World

The Cabin in the Woods is widely seen as a postmodern work,[1] and postmodernism is commonly viewed by religious leaders not only as a rejection of theism, but also as anti-humanist and nihilistic.[2] The film, particularly its ending, has thus come in for its share of the criticism aimed at postmodernist culture more generally. 'Conservative religious critics' in particular have

> attacked the ending of *Cabin* as nihilistic, based on a hatred of humanity they denominated as a hatred of God's creation. A reviewer for the highly conservative *National Catholic Register* [...] described *The Cabin in the Woods* as "literally antihuman." Suggesting that the film "cynically invites you to enjoy the destruction of people," the reviewer argued that Whedon's atheism played a significant role in his dim view of human existence.[3]

Writers who, like Poole, describe the film as 'a strange mixture of Whedon's atheism and H. P. Lovecraft's nihilism'[4] essentially accept and build on this critique. If I join them here, it is not to claim that Goddard's film symbolises postmodernism, denigrates religion or breaks a lance for progressive values. Although I believe all this to be true, none of it adequately captures the 'joyful nihilism' (Whedon's term)[5] with which the film ravages traditional (including religious) ideas of humanism. Indeed, as I hope to show in this chapter, *Cabin* is more than a critique of horror traditions, more than an attack on religion, and certainly more than an 'inoculation' (Kowalski) against fear.

If 'joyful nihilism' is the film's proffered antidote, what is the disease against which it attempts to 'inoculate'? To me the term that best describes this disorder is *fealty*, normally (and in *Cabin*, as well) denoting a vassal's sworn, generally coerced and often unthinking loyalty to an overlord. Just as the vassals of feudal times paid a yearly tithe to their masters in exchange for their protection, so the facility's Director and technicians pay a yearly blood tribute to the Ancient Ones in exchange for their continued survival. In what follows, I will use *fealty* as a comprehensive designation covering four related terms that together define the *Cabin*-verse but are individually too limited to describe the film's much larger critical target. They are *faith* (understood as a strong belief in doctrine, based on spiritual conviction rather than evidence); *religion* (understood as a system of statements made by a community about the supernatural and sacred); *mythology* (understood as a body of traditional sacred stories believed to express a profound truth and often serving as a foundation of religion); and *ritual* (understood as a ceremonial and symbolic worship rite and enactment of religious or mythological beliefs).

Cabin's arsenal of weapons, most importantly its humour and its nihilism, are firmly trained on four aspects of fealty, which will be discussed in turn.

The first is *the faith in mythical places and the attribution of mythical qualities to places*: the division of the world into the realm 'above' and 'below' reminiscent of many religious faiths; the scary woods of myth, particularly American Gothic mythology; the sobriety of the laboratory signifying an exaggerated faith in science and technology.

The second is *the faith in mythical creatures*: character caricatures (the 'Jock,' 'Scholar,' 'Virgin,' 'Whore' and 'Fool' of generic horror); symbols of dread (the monsters employed by the scientists and the Evil Gods to which they pay homage); symbols of hope (the faith in human and particularly American 'exceptionalism' as the path to salvation).

Thirdly, *the adherence to a quasi-religious ritual*, which has the effect of rendering processes inevitable and individual ethics and decision-making null and void.

And finally, *the focus on humanity at large, rather than individual people*, which has exactly the same effect.

MYTHICAL PLACES

The Cabin in the Woods stages its story on multiple levels: the Upstairs (the cabin-and-woods level), the Downstairs (the facility), below it the temple dedicated to the Ancient Ones and site of symbolic human sacrifice, and below that the fiery pit that serves as the Evil Gods' sleeping quarters. While the viewer has to wait for the film's final sequence for a glimpse of the latter two, the first two scenes, which frame the opening credits, are set Upstairs and Downstairs, without any indication how these spaces relate to one another.

The pre-credits scene, which is introduced by a close-up of a sign reading 'Enjoy a Cup of Fresh Coffee' and then treats us to a water-cooler conversation between two office workers, famously caused some viewers to walk out of the cinema, thinking they had strayed into the wrong movie. The response is understandable; the scene is meant to be disorienting. More concretely, the *place* is disorienting. The 'action' showing two middle-aged guys yammering on about female hormones and kitchen cabinets is not the point; the point is that the audience, primed by the film's title, is not where it expects to be, namely, on their way to the cabin in the woods. Our first hint that we are watching not merely a horror flick but a work of meta-horror comes to us by virtue of a setting.

For about the first third of the film, spaces both mythical and mundane set audiences on a seesaw of familiarity and disorientation, with the aim of getting viewers lost in their own woods. A large part of the film's tension is that between narrative horror and meta-horror, and that tension is, more often than not, articulated through localities. Places like the cabin, the gas station and the woods, disorienting on the narrative and diegetic level—that is, to the film's characters—are reassuringly familiar to any seasoned horror audience. Places that are most familiar to a large number of middle-class viewers in real life, like the office desk from which you temporarily escape to the water cooler or the coffee machine, are disorienting, out of context in the film we thought we were watching. All of the film's narrative spaces—from the sunny tree-lined college town that could be Anywhere, USA, to the cabin that is a distinct look-alike to any cabin in any horror flick—issue an invitation to the audience to sink into a warm, comfortingly familiar (blood-)bath. Yet the film's first scene, set in a place that is extra-diegetically familiar and diegetically incongruous, already warns us that we'll be tipped out of it, bathwater and all.

Indeed, spaces and settings become the vehicles of the film's shrewdest observations. One of them is that there is no such thing as a 'natural' space; even places shrouded in mythical lore are very much constructed. Romantic lighting and pheromones are pumped into wood clearings to encourage sexual trysts; tunnels are rigged to blow up; invisible screens block the way out. Nature is not natural; everything is engineered. This is the insight expressed by Dana (Kristen Connolly) in answer to Holden's (Jesse Williams) dreams of escape: 'It won't work. Something will happen. It'll collapse, it'll wash away... you're missing the point.' The point that Holden misses and Dana gets is that a mythical space, like the woods, is not the same as a natural space. It is made again when we see Dana dragging herself up from the lake and onto the dock, cross-cut with a beer bottle being lifted out of an ice bucket at the office party celebrating the death of her four companions, with a screen showing Dana as she collapses on the boards. Mythology, as these contrived mythical spaces hint, is not a treasure trove of sacred tales of unfathomable origin or a source of a deeper truth, but a collection of man-made stories passed down the generations for reasons that may entail the visualisation of enduring wisdoms or the justification of evil deeds.

As a mythical place, the film's Upstairs has to remain non-specific enough to be instantly recognisable to horror aficionados. The cabin, the gas station and the woods are simultaneously diegetically eerie and extra-diegetically familiar, and it is the same quality, their placelessness, that makes them so:

> Many of the places within *The Cabin in the Woods* intentionally look and feel uncannily familiar to audiences. Horror aficionados are reminded of locations in films like *The Evil Dead* (1981), *Friday the 13th* (1980), *Sleepaway Camp* (1983), *Cabin Fever* (2002), *I Spit on Your Grave* (1978), *Last House on the Left* (1972), *The Blair Witch Project* (1999), and *Wrong Turn* (2003). [...] *The Cabin in the Woods* creates this sense of placelessness by creating feelings of déjà vu; audiences feel that the places they are watching in this film could (and do) exist in any number of horror films.[6]

While the audience is thus reassured that they know where they are (falsely, to be sure, but even so), the youngsters in the film are untethered from both time and place by the same spaces. On their way to the cabin, their disorientation is still camouflaged by their pretence that they *want* to disappear off the map. 'I hope this is the right road,' says Jules (Anna Hutchison). 'It doesn't even show up on the GPS. It is unworthy of global positioning.' Answers the stoner Marty (Fran Kranz): 'That's the whole point. Get off the grid, right? No cell phone reception, no traffic cameras. Go someplace for one goddamn weekend where they can't globally position my ass, man.' The irony is, of course, that on the one hand, the youngsters very much stay on the grid (drawn for them Downstairs) while on the other, getting off the grid harbours manifest dangers.

This becomes clear when the five pull into the gas station, where their sense of dislocation becomes acute. One of horror's true mythical spaces, *Cabin*'s gas station symbolises, as it does in every horror flick, not only a warning and the last chance to turn around, but also a murky pre-civilised time. Its pumps don't accept credit cards; Mordecai (Tim DeZarn), its rude and vaguely threatening attendant, sports a biblical name and claims he has been there since some unspecified war (perhaps, as Marty sarcastically offers, the American Civil War). Even before Mordecai insults and threatens the youngsters, their jokes about the gas station ('I don't think it knows about money. I think it's barter gas') are bare of levity, full of a doom-laden heaviness that shows how badly the gas station has spooked them. Notably, too, the jokes and sarcasm point not only to spatial disorientation (their stated purpose in stopping at the gas station is to 'get directions'), but also to temporal disjunction: 'The railroad's coming through here any day now.'[7] Upstairs, there is no way of knowing what this disorientation portends; this knowledge is limited to the Downstairs, where lab technicians engineer the scenario, and the Beyond, where audiences consume it. Yet clearly the gas station is a half-way point leading not only to a place ('the old Buckner place'), but also to a time, to America's (even) more religious and (even) more savage past, a past that is now hidden deep in the woods like a rotting corpse.

Places in *The Cabin in the Woods* are mythical because they have the power to compel the narrative. The Buckners, the 'zombified, pain-worshipping backwoods idiots' who end up murdering all but Marty and Dana, are inevitable. We are, after all, at the Old Buckner Place, not the Evil Clown's Circus Tent or the Tooth-Faced Ballerina's Dance Hall.[8] That means that the office betting pool, the unforgettable scene in which the lab technicians heartlessly bet on which monsters will ultimately tear the teens apart, is really beside the point. Werewolves, go slink off with your tails between your legs. Witches, put your brooms back in the closet. Deadites, take a hike in the woods. Everything that follows is a consequence of the setting.

If the Upstairs is engineered to a fare-thee-well, the facility Downstairs seems shabby, rickety and accident-prone, hardly the kind of command centre from which you would expect the world to be saved. All equipment, while efficient enough to manipulate the mythical places Upstairs, looks decidedly dated. The coffee machine in the first scene accepts coins and features little push buttons like a 1970s cigarette machine. Later on, after the Demolition Department has failed to detonate the tunnel and nearly allowed three survivors to escape, we watch Sitterson (Richard

Jenkins) fiddle with wires to fix the problem, as if trying to hot-wire a car. As the Downstairs is ravaged by monsters, Sitterson flees to the level below not by beaming down, but by opening a trapdoor via an access code on a panel. *Cabin*'s facility is light years behind the sophisticated set-up of, say, *The Hunger Games* (released barely three weeks before *The Cabin in the Woods* and also featuring the slaughter of teens for audience entertainment),[9] which sports such space-age technology as digitally engineered monsters that can be beamed into a live scenario, force fields, toxic fogs, holographic targets, full body polishes that can erase scars, and flaming costumes. In *Cabin*, conversely, there is 'a certain decrepitude about the Cold War-era-esque bunker construction,'[10] as if the budget cuts of austerity had prevented a facility on which Earth's survival depends from keeping up with the latest technology, or even with yesteryear's. Equally unimpressive are the techies who wield this rickety equipment. Demolition misses the memo to blow the tunnel; the Chemical ('Chem') Department never gets to live down having messed up a Ritual years ago, and Sitterson and Hadley (Bradley Whitford), the Ritual's senior engineers, approach the job with the tired ennui born of years of routine. If these are the technological and people skills enlisted in the service of planetary salvation, the film implies, it's a miracle the world has endured as long as it has.

Below the Downstairs, there is only the dark space dreamed up by holy terror, Lovecraftian myth and horror conventions. Stone steps lead down to a circular temple, the floor adorned with the same religious emblem that Sitterson wears around his neck and kisses while praying to the Evil Gods, the walls emblazoned with the carved shapes of the five victims: Athlete, Scholar, Virgin, Whore and Fool. Somewhere, we know, is an industrial mechanism full of wheels and spokes that fills the chiselled outlines with blood as their originals are gruesomely killed. This temple sits at the edge of the abyss in which the Ancient Ones slumber; it is both symbolically and literally the only thing that stands between humanity and the end of the world. This, then, is the ultimate mythical place, the place about which we are told the least and below which we cannot sink, and its mythology, as recited by the facility's Director (Sigourney Weaver), is identical to the plot of any average horror flick:

> It's different in every culture. And it has changed over the years, but it has always required youth. There must be at least five. The whore. She's corrupted. She dies

first. The athlete. The scholar. The fool. All suffer and die at the hands of whatever horror they have raised, leaving the last to live or die, as Fate decides. The virgin.

In *Cabin*, the world ends by Failure of Final Girl—the virgin does not, as the formula calls for, outlive the rest of her companions. The film's refutation of horror mythology is made explicit by the fact that none of the five principal characters are a particularly good match for the clichéd horror parts assigned to them. Significantly, the two survivors and agents of the apocalypse fit their prescribed roles least well. The mismatch is, once again, expressed by recourse to setting. Of all five, Marty and Dana are the least comfortable Upstairs, least able to settle into the mythical place, least able to convince themselves that they're only there for a bit of weekend fun. Dana only joins the group hesitantly, persuaded by her friend Jules, who sees the weekend as a potential cure for Dana's ill-fated tryst with one of her professors which ended in a recent break-up, and apprehensive that Jules and her boyfriend Curt (Chris Hemsworth) are setting her up with Holden (as is indeed the case). As a result, Dana is anxious in approaching the adventure, nervous and shy around Holden, awkward and embarrassed during the Truth-or-Dare game, and visibly unable to relax at any time. For his part, Marty, that great critic of the grid, does not take well to being off it; clearly, the mythical place that has replaced it causes him intense unease. All the uncomfortable jokes at the gas station (the barter gas; the Civil War; the impending railroad; 'streets paved with actual street') are his. At the cabin, he mistakes a wolf for a moose. Outside on his walk, he is bemused by the absence of stars—another sign of displacement, and of course an echo of his earlier desire to go 'somewhere where they can't globally position my ass.' Now, looking up at the starless sky, he dimly realises that the absence of any fixed point suggesting position or enabling navigation casts humans out into the void: 'We are abandoned.'[11]

Marty's knowledge of nature may be deficient, but his cultural instinct with regard to mythical places is acute. Unlike the rest of them (except, once again, Dana), he knows a scary basement when he sees one. The cellar scene, the place where all horror myths are symbolically assembled and where the five 'choose' the manner of their destruction, again sets Marty apart from the others. Everyone else is instantly mesmerised by a particular item: Jules by an antique necklace, Holden by a music box with a dancing ballerina, Curt by a seashell conch and then a globe, Dana by Patience Buckner's diary. Marty, after a few vain attempts to get everyone to drop whatever they're playing with and go back upstairs, examines an old film reel. Of the five, he is the one who comes closest to the truth: it's all about being in someone else's movie, or, as he says in another scene, 'on a reality TV show.'

The earliest scene indicating that Dana and Marty are more profoundly misplaced in the Upstairs than the other three is the group's arrival at the film's titular mythical place, the cabin in the woods. All five get out of the vehicle, followed by a bit of uneasy banter about the sinister setting. The camera then focuses on Dana as she approaches the cabin by herself, shown ominously through a POV (point-of-view) shot from inside the cabin (fig. 5). She slowly mounts the stairs and enters alone, looking cautiously inside before fully committing herself, as if expecting an attack. A lengthy scene shows her walking around, surveying the inside with clear trepidation (fig. 6), perhaps the same trepidation with which Marty, in a cross-cut, contemplates the woods outside (fig. 7). She is all alone inside; he is all alone outside: where are the others? That Dana and Marty are visually separated from the others and isolated at first sight of the cabin, that they alone are beset by a clear sense of foreboding (just as will happen again in the cellar) shows again the greater degree of their displacement in the Upstairs. It is this insufficient alignment, this inability to suppress their sense of the mythical place's eeriness, that assigns them a dual role on the film's narrative and meta-levels, in both Upstairs and Downstairs. Because the Upstairs, their 'natural' home, has never sat well with them, they become the sole survivors, the only ones who manage to break through to what lies below, the ones who will end this Ritual and all rituals of the future.

Figure 5. Dana in the cabin's crosshairs

Figure 6. Dana explores the cabin

Figure 7. Marty contemplates the woods

How an individual relates to a place, most importantly a mythical place, becomes a central aspect of characterisation. The further down you go, the closer you are to the (your) monsters, and the more willing you are to offer up the innocent to slaughter. In the Downstairs, there is no opposition to the Ritual, no pity and no outrage, only the occasional grumblings from some powerless employee like Truman (Brian White), the Head of Security, or Lin (Amy Acker), the Head of the much-maligned Chem Department. Nobody, however, suggests calling it all off or looking for alternatives. The 'as it ever was' of Sitterson's and Hadley's prayer is synonymous with 'as it ever shall be.' Likewise, the Director informs Dana and Marty that the world can only be saved by slaughter: 'There is no other way.' The characters of the Downstairs have been unequivocally put in their place and feel at home there, and with rare exceptions they remain untroubled by twinges of either disorientation or conscience. Dana and Marty, conversely, are troubled, and it is this sense of displacement and discomfort that turns them into horror's most unusual characters, for the horror formula calls for the corruption not only of civilisation but also of character by the mythical place. This is why, as Murphy has claimed, characters who venture too far into the wilderness become savage themselves: 'The further the characters stray from "civilisation" and towards the intangible *something* that lurks at the heart of the American forest, the further they stray from their daylight, or rational "*original*" selves.'[12] But not in this case: the stoner and the Final Girl, who were only ever permitted to lead predetermined lives in the Upstairs, find their truest selves the further down they go.

MYTHICAL CREATURES

Horror films and end-of-the-world stories are a central aspect of postmodern mythology, set in mythical places inhabited by mythical creatures. A mythical creature is the inverse of a character. On one extreme end of this are the creatures in the Director's 'stable'—the zombies, the Buckners, the clowns, witches and werewolves who, or rather *which*, never possessed a real character and were always reduced to a symbolic function. The other extreme is populated by figures we perceive as 'people' (the youngsters Upstairs and the personnel Downstairs); these require some manipulation of perception to be reduced to mythical creatures. To serve as blueprints and symbols, these 'characters' must be stripped of their distinctness, their *charac*ter*istics*. This process is made obvious for the Upstairs figures and left more obscure in the Downstairs, although there is a good argument to be made—this being both a horror flick and an apocalypse-story—that nobody can be allowed to escape mythification. If the world is to end, no true character can be permitted to survive.

Non-apocalyptic reality relies on the assumption that a character is innate, primary and thus real, and that a mythical creature is something imagined, derived and thus illusory. Much horror relies on the understanding that the exact opposite is true. In one brief but highly suggestive scene, Truman, clearly not yet clued into the job, watches the Buckners at work. 'They're like something from a nightmare,' he comments with horrified fascination. 'No,' Lin corrects him: 'They're something nightmares are from. Everything in our stable is remnant of the old world. Courtesy of (*pointing down*) you-know-who.' True horror, in other words, raises questions with regard to the mythical creature's origin and therefore its level of reality. While Truman still holds on to the comforting notion that nightmare creatures are merely something we've dreamed up, Lin points out that on the contrary, our nightmares are based on a reality that we successfully suppress (most of the time).

The mythical quality of horror-creatures, then, considerably transcends their symbolism. True, mythical creatures always stand for something else: zombies symbolise the victims of technology and science (and imperialism, globalism, capitalism);[13] just as the long lineage of horror slasher killers handily symbolises the rise of the rural repressed.[14] Yet raising questions about the monster's origins adds something to its merely symbolic function because it throws doubt on *innateness itself*. If the monster is real—'something our nightmares *are from*'—then perhaps the dreamer has no greater claim on validity or reality than the monster it has dreamed up. The world we have entered now is one in which 'characters' and 'creatures' are no longer distinguished by virtue of innate authenticity. The only difference between them is that one kind of creature, like *Blade Runner*'s humans, suffers from a self-consciousness of character that insists on its principal difference—an imagined greater value derived from originality and innateness—from other creatures, like the film's replicants. In *Cabin*, as well, the characters' self-awareness (and the viewer's perception of them) relies centrally on the distinction between creatures and characters. Viewers are encouraged to presume, for example, that Curt, Holden, Dana, Jules and Marty are endowed with an innate character that transcends the parts they are assigned (the Jock, Scholar, Virgin, Whore and Fool). Only when stripped of their characteristics and reduced to their 'mythical' personas are they fit to play their assigned symbolic role, just as all the other mythical creatures do. Yet this distinction between mythical creatures and 'real' characters is broken down several times, as it is in the scene in which Dana throws herself desperately against the walls of her cube, in no way distinguishable from the many other creatures who smash against the walls of theirs. Who is to say that the other captured beasts are not beset by the same futile despair, born of the same insight of being a mere pawn, that motivates Dana in this scene?[15]

The more we rely on the successful execution of the mythical creature's assigned part, the less likely we are to see the creature playing it as a 'character,' as something endowed with innateness and the ability to act independently for the good of all. This is why we are easily able to see the mythical qualities of creatures (like zombies symbolising the victims of technology), less able to accept the mythification of creatures that appear to us like characters (such as, say, the reduction of five real-life, flesh-and-blood teens to the pre-stencilled characters of a horror flick), and even less able to see that this mythical constructedness may also apply to those 'characters' on whom we all rely to save us, like the facility's employees. Just like 'the film's monsters,' though, these saviours 'ultimately stand as avatars of an exhausted and entirely commodified pre-packaging, stacked and ready to be picked at random off the shelves of the factory archive by producers thinking only of the bottom line.'[16] Just like the zombie or the rural slasher, the employees of the Downstairs symbolise something, and scholars have had no trouble discerning what that something is: America's belief in its own exceptionalism and rightful dominion of the globe, vaguely linked with some sort of responsibility for it (in *Cabin* represented by the yearly task of pulling the world's nuts out of the potential hellfire).

Producers thinking of the bottom line have mobilised the American Saviour of the World far more often than they have found work for witches or werewolves. War movies, superhero flicks, apocalypse movies and heart-warming human-interest sagas like *The Pursuit of Happyness* (2006) all bank on the idea of Americans as exceptionally gifted, creative and determined, and of America as the one and only 'indispensable nation.'[17] Several critics, most prominently L. Andrew Cooper, have read *Cabin* as an allegory for the myth of American exceptionalism on both the narrative and the meta-level: 'One by one, other countries fail, but the Americans remain confident that their movie formulae will succeed, just as American films have long dominated global box offices.'[18] Unlike the rituals of an average war movie, superhero flick or human-interest story, though, the one in *Cabin* fails spectacularly. If we are to read this failure symbolically as the failure of American exceptionalism, the narrative end of the world is just as easily decipherable as symbolising the end of a world-*view*.

Cabin's apocalypse 'signifies not only a general incapacity to imagine a world without humans, but an American incapacity to imagine a world of the future in which the United States is no longer a global superpower.'[19] Just as there is only darkness after the Evil God's hand symbolically smashes us to smithereens, America, chronically incapable of thinking of itself as a nation like any other, will be left with nothing to replace its inflated sense of self, for 'America has not been a normal country for a long, long time.'[20]

The American Saviour of our fondest dreams, then, is no more 'real' than the ghosts, zombies and werewolves of our worst nightmares, or the Jock, Scholar, Fool, Virgin and Whore required by the Ritual. Perhaps this is the true meaning of the film's final apocalypse: the end of the world is reached when nobody and nothing retains innateness or reality, when everything and everyone is reduced to a spectre of myth and symbolic meaning.

RELIGIOUS RITUALS

Of all the themes and characters in Cabin that leave their virtual world to trespass onto extra-diegetic reality, the Ritual is the most obvious: 'the film's recasting of the horror genre's conventions as an intricate, prescribed ritual of human sacrifice performed annually ("as it ever was" [...]) is certainly as blatant an indictment of generic standardization as can be conjured.'[21] To be effective, a ritual must have mythical origins or be rooted in traditions, as well as display similarities across time and place that dwarf cultural differences. In this case, the Ritual seems to require not merely human sacrifice but specifically the sacrifice of the young by an older generation. Evidence for this includes bald statements (from the facility's Director, who informs us that the Ritual 'has always required youth'; from the film's director, who claims that 'Cabin is about youth versus adulthood');[22] genre conventions (horror viewers' apparently unquenched thirst for seeing youngsters being torn apart in the woods and the resulting tendency of horror producers to stage such scenarios);[23] even social history. In her reading of Cabin as a comment on intergenerational conflict, Karen Renner cites studies of youngster-bashing dating back all the way to 1907, showing that the older generations' dislike and distrust of the younger 'is a standard, cyclical part of history.'[24] If youngster-bashing is a time-honoured tradition ('as it ever was'), the sacrifice of the young is, in horror terms, a mere step up from there. What makes the Ritual a ritual is its *traditionalism*, its claim to mythical or religious origins and validation. A ritual shields itself from modification or transformation, from scrutiny and insubordination, by shrouding both the reasons for its existence and the identity of its perpetrators in myth: 'claiming that distant all-powerful gods demand youthful sacrificial victims dislocates evil away from tangible systems of power (ideological, bureaucratic, economic, even simian à la King Kong), relying instead on a supernatural vagueness that provided haunting community justification for murder in Shirley Jackson's "The Lottery".'[25]

Rituals, then, draw their lifeblood from the murky realms of religion and the supernatural. Even *Cabin*'s most hardened hearts, who sacrifice whores before breakfast and jocks before lunch, put on the requisite show of devoutness and fear, kissing medals and reciting little prayers. Upstairs, religious zeal is considerably more pronounced. The Buckners' worship of pain and death, as emerges from the diary of Patience Buckner (Jodelle Ferland), is cast as a quest for the True Faith.[26] Mama, she relates, could not find 'faith' even when Papa cut open her belly and stuffed hot coals inside. Patience's brothers, named (naturally) Judah and Matthew, kill travellers to show their 'devotion.' Patience in turn proves hers by allowing her arm to be cut off and eaten by the family (her 'My right arm is hacked off and et' must count as one of the film's most gruesomely memorable lines). Patience is beset by religious doubt, largely because she has a lot less fun torturing others than her male family members do: 'I want to understand the glory of the pain like Matthew, but cutting the flesh makes him have a husband's bulge, and I do not get like that.' In the end the Buckners are raised in the same way as Raimi's Deadites: by an incantation—in Raimi's case, written in Lovecraftian gibberish; in Goddard's, in Pig Latin[27]—that must be spoken 'to our spirits' by 'a believer' so the Ritual can take its ghastly course.

Once underway, there seems to be a question about what will see the Ritual through to a successful conclusion. Does the world's salvation depend on the sheer brute force exerted by the Buckners, '*our* zombified, pain-worshipping backwoods idiots,' who do, after all, have 'a 100% clearance rate'? Can salvation be obtained by mere observance, represented, perhaps, by the efficiency of bureaucrats for whom human sacrifice is just a regular Monday? Or is faith still a part of the requirement? Mordecai, the film's harbinger, essentially raises the question when he calls Downstairs, with Sitterson's and Hadley's gesticulations indicating that this event is neither rare nor welcome. On the phone, Mordecai delivers his best impression of the High Priest at the altar: 'The lambs have passed through the gate. They are come to the killing floor [...]. Their blind eyes see nothing of the horrors to come. Their ears are stopped. They are the Gods' fools. [...] Cleanse them. Cleanse the world of its ignorance and sin. Bathe them in the crimson of...' at which point he breaks off, asking in an upset tone whether he is on speakerphone. As everyone Downstairs cracks up, he delivers a warning to the unbelievers: 'Don't take this lightly, boy. It wasn't all by your numbers. The Fool nearly derailed the invocation with his insolence. The Ancient Ones see everything.' As is the case with so many scenes in *Cabin*, this one pulls double duty: a minor employee, who plays no more than a bit part in the traditional horror movie, calls Downstairs to inflate his role (and is duly rewarded by a half-hearted 'Well, you're doin' a great job out there'); and a true believer warns the faithless who see the Ritual as a mere box-ticking exercise ('By the numbers, man') that the Ancient Ones will smite them for their godlessness.[28]

That the harbinger's phone call is one of the funniest moments of the film points us to a central aspect of rituals. Precisely because rituals are among the most solemn acts imaginable, they are also among the most ridiculous. Humour emerges not only as the best way to handle the Ritual, but also as a central aspect of horror. Similar to Freud, who, a hundred years ago, identified *das Unheimliche* (the Uncanny) and *das Heimliche/Heimische* (that which is close to home and comfortingly familiar) not as opposites in terms but as nearest neighbours, Noël Carroll has proposed an adjacent kinship between horror and humour. Antithetical they may seem, but in fact horror and humour 'are so alike that indiscernibly portrayed monsters can give rise to either.'[29] Both, Carroll claims, imply a violation of norms, and both exhibit 'incongruous juxtapositions' (like the tall thin guy next to the short fat one in slapstick) or 'a sort of category error.'[30] To Carroll, what distinguishes horror from humour is nothing more than audience response:

> Ordinary moral concern for human injury is never far from our minds as we follow a horror fiction. Thus, fear is the metier of the horror fiction. In order to transform horror into laughter, the fearsomeness of the monster—its threat to human life—

must be sublated or hidden from our attention. Then we will laugh where we would otherwise scream.[31]

In this passage, Carroll assumes an incredibly moral and unspoilt horror viewer, a creature quite unrelated to the beast lusting for its regular tithe of celluloid human sacrifice. Carroll further assumes that laughing and screaming are *distinct* rather than part of the same response, a theory laid to rest comprehensively by William Paul in his book on comedy horror, *Laughing, Screaming*, and more succinctly by Peter Travers in his review of *The Cabin in the Woods*: 'Can you laugh and shriek at the same time? Yeah, baby.'[32] Failed philosophical scenes like the Harbinger's phone call demonstrate this just as well as the film's many slapstick scenes. When we see Marty whack a zombie with his giant coffee thermos bong (Travers again: 'You haven't lived until you see him use a bong as a weapon of mass destruction'), we're looking at a classic Carrollian 'category error.' A bit further on, a dismembered zombie arm saves Marty and receives, much like Mordecai, a dutiful pat on its non-existent shoulder (Marty: 'Good work, zombie arm').[33] Scenes like these confirm Carroll's view that both horror and humour rely on category errors and incongruous juxtapositions, but they also make it difficult to distinguish as neatly as Carroll does between horror and humour, laughing and screaming.

In fact, the entire film relies on mingling both. How do you exorcise a cruel ritual? By laughing it out of town. What better defence against Ancient Evil Gods than a good dose of postmodern nihilism? What better remedy against ritual's dogmatic self-righteousness than slapping it down with slapstick? The defence against the Dark Arts, to invoke a Potterism, is laughter every time; its function is to 'dismember' the film's most devout believers like a zombie arm. How seriously can we take a doomsday prophet who calls the office to brag about his job performance, mistakes his marginal role for a moment of great portent and freaks out when he realises that his pseudo-biblical drivel is audible to the entire office crew?

How seriously, for that matter, do we take a Director who mounts the stairs to the temple at five minutes to twelve, telling us how a ritual sacrifice is supposed to play out? She is, of course, all solemnity, weighed down by urgency and colossal responsibility: The End, after all, is Nigh. But then—it's Sigourney Weaver. Whedon and Goddard, in mulling over casting, were very clear that it *had* to be her: Whedon mused that 'there's nobody else who should be coming up those stairs'.[34] Goddard commented on his list of prospective actors: 'The list is one. And it's Sigourney Weaver... if she doesn't do it, I don't know, we may as well not do the movie.'[35] Why did it *have* to be Sigourney Weaver? Because anyone else might have served the horror element of the scene, but she alone could personify its humour. Only Sigourney Weaver could come up those stairs channelling Ellen Ripley,[36] an exemplar of humane behaviour who has now changed sides. Formerly a killer of monsters in defence of humanity, she now pacifies monsters by feeding them humans. From her abject position as conscientious objector and worst pain in the Company's tail, she has moved directly into its top job. Most deliciously, here is one of horror's most iconic Final Girls pleading earnestly that any deviation from the Final-Girl formula would mean the End of the World.

How do we derail the Ritual? By means of a one-armed zombified teen doing a literal hatchet job on the Final Girl (fig. 8). There goes humanity's last hope. Good work, zombie arm.

Figure 8. Patience Buckner to the rescue

Sacrosanct Humanity

Why does *Cabin* treat the ostensibly laudable goal of saving the world with such ferocious snark? Because saving the world would mean leaving it unchanged. Because saving the world would mean subscribing to the contemptible notion that it is quite alright to save humanity by sacrificing people, as if people weren't the part of humanity that matters. Because a world that considers humanity sacrosanct and people inconsequential is not worth saving.

The film's final scene pits two elemental scenarios against each other, the End and a new beginning:

> *Director.* They rise. [...] The ancient ones. The gods that used to rule the earth. As long as they accept our sacrifice, they remain below. But the other rituals have all failed. The sun is coming up in eight minutes. If you live to see it, the world will end.
>
> *Marty.* Maybe that's the way it should be. If you've got to kill all my friends to survive, maybe it's time for a change.
>
> *Director.* We're not talking about change. We're talking about the agonizing death of every human soul on the planet. Including you. You can die with them. Or you can die for them.
>
> *Marty.* Gosh, they're both so enticing.

As Marty serves up this final bit of snark, Dana trains a gun on him behind his back, having apparently fallen for the idea peddled by the Director (and every apocalypse flick): that the human race must survive at all costs, no matter how many people have to die in the cause. In the end, though, she does come to see things Marty's way. 'Humanity,' she muses at death's door. 'It's time to give someone else a chance.'

As this final line indicates, the two survivors' decision to let the world go under is motivated by more than the anger and betrayal you might understandably feel if your murder at the hands of a bunch of sanctimonious jerks is dressed up as noble martyrdom for the Greater Good. It is, rather, a philosophical decision, and one that was set up early in the film. On his way to the cabin, Marty does what he does best: roll one joint after another and rant about the state of the world. In 'The World According to Marty,' society is not, as Jules suggests with the tolerant smile of one who's heard it all before, crumbling, 'society is binding. It's filling in the cracks with concrete. Everything's filed or recorded or blogged, right? Chips in our kids' heads so they won't get lost? Society needs to crumble, we're all just too chickenshit to let it.' Before we even get to the gas station, Marty has outlined the basic alternative: either we let the world (this world) end or we grant those who run it total control over everyone, everywhere.

Cabin's final scene has exercised critics quite a bit. Champions of the continued survival of the human race have little choice but to read the conscious decision to let it all crumble as a selfish act[37] and a film that triumphantly stages the end of the world as 'a decidedly bleak and bitter work.'[38] Others have celebrated the decision as a laudable 'refusal to bow' and a 'satanic' avowal of *non servium*';[39] as a proud declaration 'that God will have to do his own dirty work' and that we 'can call God's bluff.'[40] To a third group, the scene's significance goes beyond resistance; it expresses 'the desire for a different world,'[41] one that no longer relies on the commodification (in horror: slaughter) of bodies for entertainment or economic survival. We are (here's a poke in your eye, Director) talking about change after all: 'This ending lays the groundwork for a complete transformation of humanity, society, and the world.'[42] The scholarly dispute is, of course, irresolvable; your reading of the ending will depend on your vision of the post-apocalypse. If the Director is right that nothing comes after, then humanity has been sacrificed for nothing. If Marty is right that change is possible, then whatever comes after might be better than what we had. But even if not, perhaps nothing *is* better than what we had. This may be a nihilistic statement, but it does not have to be either bleak or bitter.

Cabin's final uncertainty as to whether the world is worth saving is predicated on the question to what extent we still see humans as constituent parts of 'humanity.' Anyone capable of describing Marty's decision as choosing 'people over humanity,' as Whedon did,[43] perceives a world in which 'humanity' can be imagined as a people-free concept, a world that considers humanity sacrosanct and people expendable. Various interviews show that this idea was a major factor in both Whedon's and Goddard's thinking while they worked on the film. Goddard has compared the Downstairs to his hometown,

> Los Alamos, New Mexico, this town that exists only because it's where they set up the lab to design and build the atomic bomb. It's strange. I feel, as much as anything, that seems like *Cabin in the Woods*, particularly the downstairs aspect, because it involves very, very smart people designing weapons that are going to destroy the world.[44]

Goddard's paradox here is the reverse of Marty's, describing people—'very, very smart people,' at that—working assiduously for the destruction of humanity. Much like the ending of his film, though, his comment encapsulates the absurdity of distinguishing between the two in the first place. Whedon, likewise, has mused publicly, in a blog on the filmed murder of Du'a Khalil Aswad, about why he has 'always had a bent towards apocalyptic fiction' and, in a clearly related comment, why he has 'never had any faith in humanity.'[45] Elsewhere he states that the title of the blog in which he made these remarks—'Let's Watch a Girl Get Beaten to Death'—'could have been an alternate title for *The Cabin in the Woods*.'[46] Just like the fictitious people in *Cabin*, real-life women are customarily considered fodder to be 'inventively, repeatedly and horrifically tortured,' or 'at the very least, expendable.' That people, most particularly women, are routinely savaged in this fashion makes it difficult to believe in humanity:

> Faith in God means believing absolutely in something with no proof whatsoever. Faith in humanity means believing absolutely in something with a huge amount of proof to the contrary. We are the true believers. [We] codify our moral structure, without the Sky Bully looking down telling us what to do.[47]

True faith in humanity, in other words, is letting go of the idea of human 'exceptionalism,' of the conceit that humanity will and must endure, in life and afterlife. 'We want to believe that we'll be able to go on forever,' Whedon continues, 'that when we die there will be ice cream and cake and we'll play hooky every day.' But maybe we shouldn't put so much pressure on poor old humanity, let alone on people: 'You eventually get to a place where you realize you aren't the point. [...] You can get to a place [...] where you realize that when your time is up, the worms are hungry… and kinda cute.' Acknowledging the cuteness of the worms, and more importantly recognising that you aren't the point, is, Whedon concludes, 'a joyful nihilism that refuses to surrender to despair… even if the weekend ends with giant evil gods rising.'[48] 'I wish I could have seen them,' says Dana, adding her own wistful pinch of joyful nihilism. Counters Marty, refusing to surrender to despair: 'I know. That would have been a fun weekend.'

Whedon's cosmology is simple: humanity isn't the point. Some writers, both philosophers and literary authors, have tried to tell us this, and we call them 'horror' writers because they do. Of Eugene Thacker's three ways of thinking about the world—the world-for-us, the world-in-itself, and the world-without-us—only the last is perceived as a vision of horror, just as Lovecraft's stories are considered tales of 'cosmic horror' because they propose that humanity is not at the centre of the cosmos.[49] Our way of countering the insignificance of humans is to endow collective 'humanity' with an exaggerated exceptionalism now sufficiently familiar to be expressed in soundbites (God's Greatest Creation; Alone Among Earth's Creatures to be Ensouled; Made in God's image; Masters of the Universe; Hope of Heaven; World Without End; the Greater Good; Survival Imperative, and so on and so forth).

The moment individuals are no longer accorded the same degree of sanctity and significance as 'humanity' is the moment we are looking at humanity without people. If rituals, myths and religion facilitate savaging people in the name of humanity, then nihilism is the only way out. If nihilism is a way of injecting people back into 'humanity,' then we should ask why we so often employ religious rituals as the means to deny people the inviolability that we claim for 'humanity' as a matter of course.[50] This is perhaps the greatest philosophical paradox expressed in *The Cabin in the Woods*: that respect for human life begins with the denial that humanity is sacrosanct.

Notes

1. So noted by Canavan, 'Nightmares' para. 9; Lockett 135; McDonald para. 2; Derrick King para. 13.
2. See, for example, the contribution by Jim Leffel and Dennis McCallum, particularly their sections 'Postmodernism Means the Death of Truth' and 'Postmodern Antihumanism.'
3. Poole 215.
4. Poole 213.
5. Poole 213, citing Whedon.
6. Wagner para. 11.
7. For a discussion of the gas station, see Lockett 130 and Wagner para. 7.
8. As pointed out by Lockett 131.
9. On the similarities between the two films, see Parker 196–7.
10. Weyant para. 7.

11. On this scene, see the comments by Wagner para. 9.
12. Murphy 1 (emphases original).
13. As pointed out by Day, among many others.
14. Clover 27–30; Parrish para. 11.
15. As noted by Blouin, 'Growing Global Darkness' 92.
16. Woofter and Stokes para. 9.
17. The phrase was popularised by Madeleine Albright as Secretary of State, who began to use the phrase more frequently from 1998 in defence of America's coercive Iraq diplomacy; see Zenco.
18. Cooper para. 4. For a further reading of *Cabin* as an allegory of American exceptionalism, see Giannini, 'BellyBeast'; on American exceptionalism as a theme in US films, see Everett.
19. Cooper para. 23.
20. Cooper para. 24.
21. Parrish para. 9.
22. Richardson 63–5 on the sacrifice of youth theme; the citation from Goddard on 64.
23. On ritual sacrifice as a central aspect of the film and its metacommentary on the genre, see, among others, Renner; Parker; Moldenhauer, 'Pigs' 25; Richardson 63–5; Starr note 4; Whitty; Woofter and Stokes para. 3; Metz para. 22; Lockett 131, 137.
24. Renner, see particularly 113–19; the citation on 118.
25. Metz para. 22.
26. On the Buckners, see Lockett 131.
27. The incantation as offered in the film reads: 'Dolor supervivo caro. Dolor sublimis caro. Dolor ignio animus.' A rough translation of this ungrammatical passage might be: 'Pain outlive flesh. Pain elevated flesh. Pain ignite soul.' Rendering this into a grammatically more correct version might yield the following: 'Dolor carnem supervivit. Dolor carnem levat. Dolor animum ignit' ('Pain survives the flesh. Pain relieves the flesh. Pain sets the soul to burn'). A brief analysis of the incantation has been offered by an anonymous commentator on reddit, 'I don't know much Latin, but I'm pretty sure the Latin in *The Cabin in the Woods* is wrong.'
28. On the distinction between the devout and the faithless, see also Parker 204.
29. Carroll 147.
30. Carroll 152–4.
31. Carroll 158.
32. In his review of *The Cabin in the Woods* in *Rolling Stone*.

33. For an analysis of this scene as slapstick, see Parrish para. 13.
34. Quoted in Pascale 324.
35. Goddard's comment in 'We Are Not Who We Are.'
36. Ripley appeared in the *Alien* franchise (1979–97, dir. Scott, Cameron, Fincher, Jeunet). On the Director/Ripley intertextuality, see Starr, among many others.
37. See, for example, the following assessments by Renner ('Ultimately the choice is [...] a conflicted one, incredibly generous while also exceptionally selfish, meaning, as it does, the end of existence for everyone who isn't a "friend" as well,' 121–2); Paik ('it is hard to suppress the thought that the two friends arrive at it [their decision] with inordinate haste [...] the principle that children are innocent of adult vices and should not be punished for the wrongdoings of their elders does not factor at all in their deliberations [...] it appears that humankind is annihilated in a fit of thoughtlessness,' 112); Kowalski, who suggests that Marty probably should have sacrificed himself to save Dana and the world (Chapter 8 in *Joss Whedon as Philosopher*); and Metz, who has considered the ending 'more pointless than enabling' (para. 13). On the final choice, see also Parrish's analysis of utilitarianism in paras 2–3.
38. Woofter and Stokes para. 3.
39. Lockett 136–7.
40. McDonald para. 16.
41. Derrick King has read the ending as a Utopian and dialectical critique of the commodification of people in corporate capitalism; the quotation on para. 24.
42. Mayo 253.
43. On the commentary track of the DVD version of the film; cited, among others, in Renner 121.
44. The statement by Goddard in a *Fangoria* interview with him and Whedon, cited by Cooper para. 25.
45. Both in Whedon's blog comment 'Let's Watch a Girl Get Beaten to Death.' On Whedon's comments in this blog, see also Giannini, 'Charybdis.'
46. Quoted in Parker 208.
47. From Whedon's acceptance speech for the Harvard Humanist Society's award for 'Outstanding Lifetime Achievement in Cultural Humanism' in 2009, cited in Lockett 122–3.
48. All quotations from Whedon's acceptance speech, cited in Poole 224.
49. See Poole 214 for Lovecraft's tales of dread. Jared Richardson has offered a convincing application of Thacker's thought experiment to *The Cabin in the Woods*, see especially 72–8.

50. See Kowalski's conclusion: 'There is a level of maturity to seeing the smaller picture. There is also a level at which you understand the meaning of the microcosm of your own personal relationships as being the actual world. [...] The basic moral message of the film is that "people are more important than humanity"' (the inserted quotation is Whedon's; *Joss Whedon as Philosopher* 186).

Chapter 3: Either v. Or: The Puppets' Choice

> *When I argue, then, that we might do well to attempt what is surely impossible—to withdraw our allegiance, however compulsory, from a reality based on the Ponzi scheme of reproductive futurism—I do not intend to propose some 'good' that will thereby be assured... We might rather, figuratively, cast our vote for 'none of the above.'*
>
> Lee Edelman[1]

When Roger Ebert called *Cabin* 'essentially an attempt to codify free will,'[2] he simultaneously defined the film as a philosophical work and touched upon a subject that philosophers and pop philosophers have taken to mean different things. In philosophy, there is an ongoing debate about free will that pits compatibilists, who hold that free will and determinism are compatible, against incompatibilists, who claim that they aren't. Both arrive at opposite conclusions by way of an identical argument. Compatibilists define free will as nothing more than an article of personal faith, granting humans mental freedom in a deterministic universe. Incompatibilists similarly argue that free will is an illusion born of a strong desire for freedom and control, making determinism the only reality. This difference that makes no difference rests on a distinction that is more meaningful: that between freedom of will and freedom of action. If free will does not result in freedom of action, then humans, even with the best (free) will in the world, have no influence on their future.[3] Dystopian novelists from Huxley in *Brave New World* (1932) onwards have proposed the exact opposite, namely the existence of freedom of action in the absence of free will. Humans, they claim, would

> have a great deal of everyday freedom to do whatever we wanted, yet our freedom of *will* would be severely limited. We would be free to *act* or to choose *what* we willed, but we would not have the ultimate power over what it is that we willed. Other persons would be pulling the strings, not by coercing or forcing us to do things against our wishes, but by manipulating us into having the wishes they wanted us to have.[4]

To a greater or lesser degree, all three positions, compatibilist, incompatibilist and dystopian, argue for the reality of determinism. If humans are endowed with free will coupled with the inability to enact it, determinism is real. If human freedom of action exists but is made meaningless by an inability to will that action freely, then 'determinism poses no real threat to free will, or at least to any kind of freedom or will "worth wanting".'[5]

If academic philosophy projects a gloomy outcome, attitudes tend to be more cheerful in the pop branch of the discipline, which views free will and determinism as antithetical and free will as automatically implying freedom of action. To this conceptual casserole, the pop philosopher adds another ingredient—*choice*—and declares it to be central to the entire dish: 'Free will is about choosing.'[6] 'Expert opinions,' experts declare, 'have yielded a wide and controversial assortment of conceptions of free will, but laypersons seem to associate free will more simply with making choices.'[7] Choice becomes the glue that binds together ideas strictly separated in traditional philosophy: 'Laypersons cognitively associate free will with the concept of choice,' from where they go on to 'perceiving actions as choices' and 'associating choice with freedom.'[8] Where a philosopher perceives complex interactions, a pop philosopher sees only an equals sign—freedom of will equals freedom of action, and both are embodied by choice.

That *Cabin* is a philosophical film was obvious not only to Ebert,[9] but it is less evident where on the sliding scale between pop and profound the film comes down. What I would like to propose in this chapter is that it's not a case of 'either-or' but a case of 'as-well-as' (in fact, part of the film's point is to attack either-or as a false choice). Certainly, *Cabin* is profound as a philosophical film, for it refuses resolutely to equate free will with freedom of action. Equally clearly, *Cabin* behaves like a pop-philosophical film, for its surface chatter is all about that thing that the pop philosopher is most likely to confuse with freedom: choice. And even more assuredly, *Cabin* is a dystopia in the best Huxleyan and Orwellian tradition, portraying a world inhabited by people who do not have the ultimate power over what it is that they will. Other persons are pulling the strings.

'We chose,' whispers Dana despondently in the glass elevator, and then promptly corrects herself: 'They made us choose. They made us choose how we die.' That the two statements contradict each other and that the second is in itself absurd should be self-evident, for a coerced choice is no choice at all. As Derrick King has pointed out, 'a choice cannot really be undertaken freely when the "game"—or, more precisely, the social matrix constituting the field of possible choices one can make—has been "rigged" in advance.'[10] King goes on to read *Cabin* 'as a political allegory for the way in which freedom is, under global capitalism, radically overdetermined by mechanisms of ideological, electronic, and biological control.'[11] Universal control over human behaviour was apparently also at the forefront of Whedon's mind:

> we are all controlled, we are all experimented upon, and we are all dying from it. And we are completely unaware of it. We are taught not to be kind. We are taught not to be forward-thinking. We are taught not to be as much as we can be. We are taught to be insecure. We are taught to be subservient. We are taught to be aggressive. And we are taught to buy, buy, buy. … And these are things that are going on every day, all the time, in everybody's life.[12]

If the game is sufficiently rigged, we all live in a deterministic universe, leaving us both with the illusion that we're endowed with free will and unaware of how limited the choices we're offered actually are. This is the belated understanding that drives Dana to throw herself against her glass cage in the same despair felt by the other creatures entrapped in theirs; this is the insight encapsulated in Marty's single whispered word: 'Puppeteers.'

The way in which a society of puppeteers and puppets functions is precisely as described in many a dystopian novel. You are apparently free to choose what you will, and to act on that choice. You interpret your will as free because nobody is forcing you to do anything against your will. But all the while, you are being manipulated to have the wishes that someone else wants you to have. Even worse, you are being manipulated to become unaware of options that someone else deems undesirable. The philosophical *Cabin*-verse goes well beyond limiting choices or manipulating people's ability to act on a choice they have made; it attacks the ability to will in the first place. To illustrate: imagine you are in a hotel in the summer, in a room on the 35th floor equipped with security windows to prevent suicides. You can choose to turn the air conditioner on or off. You cannot choose to open the window. A *Cabin*-esque level of control does not merely require you to stop wanting to open the window, or to stop wondering why you can't, or to be unable to have that little internal debate whether you agree or disagree with the anti-suicide measure. A *Cabin*-esque level of control is reached when you are unable to imagine why anyone would ever want to open a window, when you are, as Whedon put it, 'completely unaware' that windows open and that opening one is something you might want to do. Opening the window has become a blind spot in your mind, an option erased by those who are in charge of shaping it and the choices allowed to occur to it.

This indirect but actually far more comprehensive level of control is what makes the bizarre insistence of *Cabin*'s scenario engineers that their victims are free to choose their fate both more understandable and more pernicious. Truman, the security guard with the twitchy conscience, points out that the game is rigged, and is rewarded with the stock lecture:

> *Truman.* How can you wager on this when you control the outcome?
>
> *Hadley.* No, we just get 'em in the cellar. They take it from there.
>
> *Sitterson.* No, they have to make the choice of their own free will. Otherwise the system doesn't work. It's like the harbinger. It's this creepy old fuck, practically wears a sign 'You will die.' Why do we put him there? The system. They have to choose to ignore him, and they have to choose what happens in the cellar. Yeah, we rig the game as much as we need to, but in the end, they don't transgress…
>
> *Hadley.* They can't be punished.

The job, then, is not to eliminate free will, it is to limit the will's capacity to want anything outside of the choices you prescribe. The job is to play by the rules laid down by 'the system' (Ancient Evil Gods; capitalism; take your pick) and arrive at a predetermined outcome. The outcome is predetermined when you have successfully made all options leading to other outcomes unthinkable to your puppets, who remain, within the permitted menu of choices, free to will whatever they want.

Cabin finds a relatively straightforward narrative means to express this philosophical paradox: turning characters into types. All five are shoehorned into parts corresponding to horror archetypes and bearing little or no relation to their original character; 'deliberately positioned,' as Day has put it, 'both as an archetype and as a subversion of type.'[13] Marty, no fool he, is turned into the Fool. Jules, assigned the role of the Dumb Blonde, is actually neither. Originally a brunette and pre-med, she morphs into the Whore, leaving Dana to play the Whore's polar opposite, the Virgin, presumably because there is no other female part left. Curt, a sociology major on full scholarship and quite capable of having a non-lecherous academic discussion with a girl in her underwear, mutates into the Athlete and obnoxiously randy alpha dog, while the actual athlete, Holden, is turned into a bespectacled Scholar translating Latin. That the labels they are assigned are completely out of character, theoretically landing the team Downstairs with a tougher job, is mystifying. Why not, we might ask, assign Curt, who gives Dana strategic reading advice in the first scene, the Scholar role? Why not let Holden play what he is, 'the best hands on the team' (according to Curt)? Why is Jules with her stable love relationship more eligible to play the Whore than Dana, who has recently emerged from an illicit tryst with a married professor? Of course, as has been pointed out, the contrasts between original and assigned character serve to point out the ludicrousness of horror clichés,[14] to which we might add that the greater the rift between assigned character and original, the more impressive the display of control over their behaviour. If a bunch of bureaucrats can transform an adulteress into a Virgin or two smart, studious, and thoughtful people into Dumb Blonde and Dumb Jock, they can presumably turn a frugal person into a shopping mall zombie, or a faithfully married down-and-out war veteran into the groupie of a draft-dodging casino billionaire on his third trophy wife.

The vast space between the characters' assigned personas and their pre-tampering personalities generates discomfort. 'For them to serve their purpose,' Day writes, 'they must be recognizable as an ideal type, but it must also be clear that something is amiss.'[15] The tension between the two raises questions: can a type ever act against type? Does a character struggle against being turned into a cliché, and if so, for how long?

In the very first scene featuring the five, Curt holds up a pair of sociology textbooks to Jules and shouts accusingly: 'Who gave you these? Who taught you about these?' Jules, aggrieved, shoots back: 'I learned it from you, okay? I LEARNED IT FROM WATCHING YOU!' and runs out of the room. The scene sends up a public service announcement (PSA) anti-drugs ad from the depth of the 1980s War on Drugs, which shows a father confronting his son with his stash of dope and receiving the same response to the same question.[16] The message to the viewer is clear: brace yourself for lots of spoofing. The point is also to provide the audience with a glimpse of characters who are still a cut above clichés, who are in fact able to recognise and lampoon them—a Jules not yet dumbed down by the chemicals in her hair dye, a Curt not yet propelled by pheromones to trade his magnificent brains for an overdose of brawn. Without transition, Jules and Curt shift from a smart, quick-witted and playful couple in one scene to brainless and oversexed Jock and Whore in the next. Horror conventions leave no room for the subtleties of measured characterisation and development, and it is once again Marty, the prophetic fool, who points this out. 'Why is Jules suddenly a celebu-tard?' he asks Dana, who refuses to see anything wrong. 'And since when does Curt pull this alpha-male bullshit? I mean, he's a sociology major. He's on full academic scholarship, and now he's calling his friend an egghead?'

If Jules and Curt are turned upside down in no time, the switch from character to type is more complicated for the film's second couple, Dana and Holden. Unlike Jules and Curt, they are granted fleeting moments of awareness. When Holden muses 'Weird how it comes back,' as he translates the diary's Latin passage, and when Dana tells Holden that she's not ready for more than a kiss ('I don't wanna… I mean I've never… I don't mean "never"…'), both experience a momentary disconnect between character and cliché.[17] That Dana, briefly forgetting all about her adulterous affair, can state without consciously lying that she's never had sex shows that the cliché is gaining ground. Both are turning into the roles they've been assigned to play because they begin to believe, however fleetingly, that this is who they are.

Just as we are offered a brief glimpse of the original Curt and Jules in the first Upstairs scene, Dana's and Holden's original characters materialise in a scene that doubles as a commentary on free will. Holden's room features a gruesome painting showing snarling beasts and humans tearing innocent animals to shreds, with a mysterious figure sporting a long knife looming in the distance. Horrified, he takes it down, revealing a one-way mirror showing Dana undressing in the adjoining room (fig. 9). This is Holden's first test of character, or, in the language of Downstairs, his first chance to 'transgress.' He passes it with flying colours, banging on the wall to alert Dana to stop undressing. He shows her the mirror and offers to switch rooms, which she gratefully accepts. The sequence ends with an exact role reversal: Dana in her new room watches Holden undress through the mirror (fig. 10), fights a moment of temptation, and then hastily hangs the picture back on the wall to preserve his privacy. Her verbal double-take upon taking in the awful picture is identical to his: 'Yeah, I don't think so.' In the end, she covers the painting with a blanket.

Figure 9. Dana as an invitation to 'transgress'

Figure 10. Holden as an invitation to 'transgress'

In rejecting both sex and gore, Dana and Holden behave with considerably greater integrity than either the scenario managers Downstairs or an average horror audience.[18] The mirror scene is also a figurative mirror scene for another aborted striptease in the film, the moment when Jules is about to unbutton her blouse. Hadley and Sitterson anticipate this event with all the listlessness with which one might watch a TV ad for toilet paper: 'Okay, baby, let's see some boobies.' / 'Show us the goods.' Their decidedly bored tone indicates that they really couldn't care less about seeing Jules naked, but they, too, have to play their assigned parts, that of the horror producers charged to give audiences what they came for. When Truman expresses his disgust, he is admonished: 'We're not the only ones watching, kid. [...] Gotta keep the customer satisfied.' In the world of horror where sex always equals a death sentence, the baring of boobs plays a two-fold role. Taken by itself it titillates the watchers—those Downstairs (or at least those less jaded than Hadley and Sitterson), the Ancient Ones, and, of course, the horror audience. Taken as a generic marker, it buttresses horror's logic that victims are complicit in their deaths—if you don't transgress, you can't be punished.

The mirror scene, then, is clearly an invitation to Dana and Holden to 'transgress,' and one that is supposed to end differently; as Hadley makes clear, the room change occasioned by Holden's decency comes as a surprise to the Downstairs team. That Dana and Holden fail to transgress turns what should have been a stock scene of horror into a comment on the idea of free will. When the game is rigged to such a degree that your 'choices' are down to either v. or—in this case, the classic horror options of either voyeurism, represented by Dana's and Holden's aborted striptease, or violence, represented by the painting—exercising your free will means saying: none of the above. The mirror scene is a rare moment in the film when things do not go according to the plan hatched Downstairs. As such, it not only 'mirrors' Jules and Curt getting down to business in the forest, but more crucially foreshadows the final apocalypse, which is, after all, caused by a couple being offered an either-or alternative ('You can die with them. Or you can die for them.') and opting for none of the above.

The rules laid down by the Downstairs engineers both spell out the complicity requirement of horror, where characters always 'deserve' their fate, and degrade the idea of free will to a mere rationalisation for the killing.[19] The way *Cabin* handles the paradox is not merely by pointing out the absurdity of the horror genre's moral universe, but by adding that transgression and punishment are actually not linked in any way. Characters don't have to be 'pure' to escape the horror script written for them, nor do they have to 'transgress' to be punished. In the same scene in which Dana and

Holden valiantly resist the temptations of sex and violence, both are revealed to be less than perfect:

> *Dana.* I'm not looking for… but I'm still grateful that you're not a creep.
>
> *Holden.* Let's not jump to any conclusions there, alright? I had kind of an internal debate about showing you the mirror. Shouting on both sides, blood was spilled.
>
> *Dana.* So, you're bleeding internally?
>
> *Holden.* Pretty bad.
>
> *Dana.* Well, Jules is pre-med. You should probably talk to her.
>
> *Holden.* Um. Oh. Okay.

Holden is decent and honest, but not perfect—he admits that he was tempted to watch. Dana, for her part, commits a worse sin in this scene: telling him that Jules will 'cure' his sexual temptation suggests that Jules will sleep with anyone. This is another moment in which the assigned type temporarily trips up the original character. Dana brands her best friend a 'whore' and then withdraws from the scene, sporting a puzzled expression that clearly implies 'I can't believe I just said that,' just as she will later appear mystified at her own nonsensical claim to be a virgin.

Dana and Holden, tempted but decent, confused yet also aware, are central to the film's project to unmask the Complicity Rule that governs both the world Downstairs and the world of horror as manifest nonsense. Holden will die without committing a sin of any kind. The worst Dana could be accused of—unless we count an affair in which she was not the driving force, which clearly caused her pain, and which ended before the film's first scene—is her implicit betrayal of Jules. And yet Dana (who in the moral world of horror might be judged less 'guilty' than randy Curt, lascivious Jules or stoner Marty) is ultimately responsible for setting the horror scenario in motion. She is the first to approach the cabin; she is the first through the door. She is the first to go down to the cellar, and it is the item she selects that raises the Buckners. Why, of all possible choices, is Dana cast as the film's Agent of Doom? Because her selection demonstrates that 'transgression' does not imply corruption. The Complicity Rule requires neither real immorality nor actual misdeeds, let alone something as overstrung as 'evil.' Momentary distractions and fleeting temptations (even those that require a fair amount of rigging to produce) are quite sufficient to warrant agonising torture followed by the death penalty.

Chemical and mechanical manipulation, as the contrast between the couples shows, works at different speeds on different people. Curt and Jules succumb quickly (how practical for the engineers, since the rules call for the Whore to be dispatched first), Holden and Dana more slowly. Marty, the perennial stoner, escapes much of this manipulation because, as the Head of the Chem Department realises belatedly, 'the prep team missed one of the kid's stashes. Whatever he's been smoking's been immunizing him to all our shit.' The delightful scene where he whacks a zombie with his bong is thus really no more than a literal image of how he's been beating them all along. Marty's greater awareness may further be helped by the fact that he is the odd man out, unpartnered and thus unlikely to be distracted by the sexual opportunities the weekend might provide. He is also the odd man out in the sense that unlike the rest of them, he initially seems to fit his assigned part best. His entry into the film shows him driving up with the window rolled down, puffing huge clouds of pot smoke outside from an enormous bong. He locks his car by pushing the lock-button through the open window and checks twice whether the door is securely locked, all the while lecturing his friends, who watch all this with horrified amusement, that cops will never pull over a man with a giant bong because 'They fear this man. They know he sees farther than they and he will bind them with ancient logics.' Not the sharpest knife in the drawer, then, or so we think.

In fact, Marty's instincts are sharp throughout and rarely let him down. Whereas everyone else is upset, offended and fearful at the gas station, Marty is agitated by the encounter in a far more fundamental way. The same elemental dread resurfaces when he first lays eyes on the cabin. He retains a healthy distrust of dank cellars and vociferously objects to reading the inscription: 'I'm drawing a line in the fucking sand here. Do not read the Latin!' While everyone else does not hear but obeys the subliminal messages piped in from Downstairs, Marty hears them as whispered commands ('Read it. Read it out loud!') and argues back. Alone in his room, he hears a suggestive whisper instructing him to go for a walk so he can be dispatched in the forest, which prompts an outburst: 'You think I'm a puppet, huh? You think I'm a puppet, gonna do a little fucking puppet dance! I'm the boss of my own brain, so give it up!' On the heels of this: 'I'm gonna go for a walk.' Even Marty, then, although far more attuned to what is actually happening, is not immune. He, too, can be distracted, not by sex like the other four but by the stoner's perennial bugbear, the munchies. When he warns Dana that Curt and Jules are behaving in an uncharacteristic fashion, he lays his finger on the wound, whispering to himself: 'Puppeteers.' Dana repeats the word, disbelievingly—'Puppeteers?'—upon which Marty, his insight instantly forgotten, asks eagerly: 'Pop Tarts? Did you say you have Pop Tarts?'

His 'logics' temporarily derailed, he nevertheless arrives at the correct conclusion: 'We are not who we are.' It is, like so many of Marty's statements, philosophy disguised as stoner gobbledygook. Marty is a philosopher in the sense that he thinks at an abstract level about the nature of human thought, the nature of the universe, and the links between them—as he tells his friends, 'I have a theory about this.' Even the silly formulation 'ancient logics,' with its twin allusion to the epoch in which philosophy originated and to one of its sub-disciplines, hints at Marty's philosopher status. His 'We are not who we are' sounds asinine but is a philosophical assessment that describes not merely an inability to act but an inability to continue to *be*. It is shorthand for a theory of free will, suggesting not merely loss of control over one's actions but a loss of essential character, and with it any ability to will anything that falls outside of the parameters programmed into the type that has replaced it.

Hadley and Sitterson, those stalwart champions of free will, are actually the best examples for its limitations and for the vast disparity between freedom of will and freedom of action. Nominally in control, they are, much like their victims, only free to act within the coordinates set by their roles. Entrusted with the most important job in the world, they are bored rigid by it; nothing gets a rise out of them until the Apocalypse is at hand. The sight of Jules's bare breasts, eagerly anticipated by everyone else in the office (fig. 11), stirs them to no more than the requisite line—'Show us the goods'—delivered in a tone that is best described as near-comatose (fig. 12). When everyone else panics about the possibility of failure and resulting Armageddon, like Lin who reminds them in a worried tone that it's now down to Japan and them, they brush it off. 'It's going to be a long weekend if everyone's that puckered up,' sighs Hadley. Until it all goes to hell, they behave exactly like white-collar employees hired to do a paint-by-numbers job within a system of strictly enforced rules. They design the scenario, but even they are not granted the authority to colour outside of the lines.

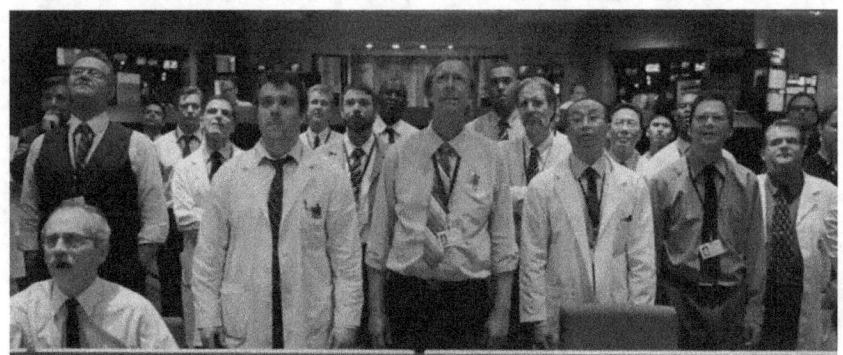

Figure 11. *The Downstairs crew anticipate the unbuttoning of a blouse*

Figure 12. *Hadley and Sitterson anticipate the unbuttoning of a blouse*

Hadley and Sitterson's profoundly predetermined work environment, their lack of authority and creativity, and not least their apathy all contrast sharply with their nominal role as Saviours of the World. But they are also, even more than Dumb Jock and Dumb Blonde, exemplars for what happens to people when they are unfree to will anything on their own. Imaginations suffer; brain-rot sets in; adults magically regress to the age of five. There is a distinct disconnect between degrees of emotion and the occasions that arouse them; the greatest horrors elicit no response; the most intense feelings are triggered by infantile occasions. Seeing human beings horribly killed elicits neither shock nor pity, but when Hadley's favourite monster, the Merman, is not selected to dispatch the five, Hadley sinks into abject sadness, even borderline depression. 'He [Curt] had the conch in his hand,' he whines to Sitterson, sounding for all the world like a toddler who's just been told that Mummy won't buy him yet another toy. 'I am *never* gonna see a merman. *Ever.*'[20] Positive emotions like joy or amusement, on the rare occasion that Hadley or Sitterson express them, are inevitably linked to petty pursuits, like making fun of the weirdo (Mordecai on speakerphone), basking in the sycophantic praise of lower-ranked employees at the party, and, of course, getting hammered (the welcome arrival of booze unceremoniously cuts short Hadley's five seconds of sympathy for Dana, who is being mauled on the screen). That such characters might ever think about their role in the 'system' or impose their will on it in any way is inconceivable, and this is so because the 'system' does not allow for free will in any meaningful sense, but assigns the term a specific role, as it does to everything and everyone else. For the puppets, free will is ensnared in the straitjacket of either v. or 'choices'; for the puppeteers, free will is diminished to playing a bit part in the Complicity Rule so it can serve as the justification for slaughter.

Cabin's ending is not unthinkable because it shows the End of the World, which has, after all, been imagined over and over in any number of B-genre films. The part of the final scene that really boggles the mind is not the Apocalypse but the vision of two people exercising their free will. Even more unimaginably, they do it in a way that transcends the narrow confines of pop philosophy, which declares free will to be all about 'choice.' Having been forced to 'choose' the manner of their deaths, the two survivors arrive at the temple with a new-found clarity about what choices are worth. Dana is a bit behind Marty, but in the end, she, too, realises that either v. or—in this case, dying either with or for humanity—is no more than a puppet's choice. Their joint decision, then, cannot be described as a choice, since it refuses both the either and the or. Rather, it is a proclamation: None of the Above. Unlike a 'choice' between either and or, None of the Above, an approximation of free will, does not gun for a specific outcome. Unlike a choice, free will refuses to subordinate itself to freedom of action; when a choice is refused, freedom of will and freedom of action part company, leaving free will to stand on its own. Dana and Marty, in fact, do not really exercise theirs until they have run out of both choices and possibilities for action. Their decision defines free will as the freedom *not* to choose, as the imagination of a world beyond predetermined choices, and as the wish to bring it about. The apocalypse, in this Utopian reading,[21] means not the End of the World, merely the end of a world not worth living in—one that degrades people to serve as either puppets or puppeteers, as either cogs in the machine or stereotypes that can be strong-armed into a sub-human role, only to be thrown away because they are no more than that. When Dana and Marty bid good riddance to that world, they convey both a simple assertion and an unimaginable freedom—the freedom that comes from the refusal of choices designed by someone else, and the freedom that comes from the refusal to make any demands on the future.

The Cabin in the Woods confronts us with two kinds of horror, 'the generic sense of characters being stalked and killed by implacable, unstoppable monsters; and the horror of losing one's personal agency to the ministrations of a malevolent higher power.'[22] That the second kind of horror is not safely imprisoned in the narrative is readily apparent; 'by the end,' Roger Ebert wrote in his review, 'we realize we're playthings of sinister forces.' Yet even those of us who understand that the film's philosophical tentacles are coming for us are not about to let them get to us beyond the safe and indirect manner in which we 'identify' with fictional characters. 'The movie wants us to re-examine and rearrange its constituent parts; in fact, it demands that we do so. In this re-examination we become the unknowing sacrificial victims (sometimes), and we are the cold-hearted guardians of society (sometimes).'[23] Identification serves to remind us that the film has something to say that should matter to us as well as the five teens, but it still offers us no more than another either v. or: feel free to imagine yourself as either puppet or puppeteer.

Can we envision anything beyond this? If the apocalypse of the final scene symbolises not the End of the World but 'the desire for a different world,'[24] then the film's ending calls for more than mere identification with either puppet or puppeteer. It calls for the realisation that like both of them, we are not '"outside" ideology and power' and therefore are never really '"free" as such.'[25] It invites us to think the unthinkable: that we might withdraw our allegiance from the Ponzi scheme of puppets' choices, and begin to desire a world in which nobody pulls our strings. It urges us to reject choice and embrace imagination as if our free will depended on it. For a film that has so often been panned as unimaginative schlock horror, it's really not a bad philosophy. Reading the worst of these reviews,[26] you could be forgiven for thinking that the film never achieved anything beyond employing hundreds of people—including, apropos of nothing, eight puppeteers.

Notes

1. Edelman 4.
2. Ebert in the *Chicago Sun-Times*.
3. The statements in this paragraph are a brief summation of aspects of the works by Kane; Baer, Kaufman and Baumeister; Bergson; Blumenau; Caruso; and Williams.
4. Kane, *A Contemporary Introduction to Free Will* 2 (emphases original).
5. Kane, *A Contemporary Introduction to Free Will* 7.
6. This is the title of Feldman, Baumeister and Wong's essay on the layperson's faith in a strong link between choice and free will.
7. Feldman, Baumeister and Wong 239.
8. Feldman, Baumeister and Wong 239.
9. See Kowalski's chapter on the film in *Joss Whedon as Philosopher*.
10. Derrick King para. 1.
11. Derrick King para. 1.
12. Whedon, Goddard and Bernstein 274–5.
13. Day (unpag.).
14. This speculation is offered by Graves; Giannini, 'Charybdis' para. 11; Day; Fuchs; Lockett 132–3; Mayo 239; Parrish paras 17–19; Renner 120; Sessarego.
15. Similarly pointed out by Metz para. 16.
16. The original ad, which can be viewed on YouTube, was part of a large-scale anti-narcotics campaign by the Partnership for a Drug-Free America and has been spoofed numerous times (see https://en.wikipedia.org/wiki/I_learned_it_by_watching_you!).
17. On this scene, see Giannini, 'Belly' 91.
18. As has been pointed out by Kowalski; Cooper para. 9; Parrish paras 26 and 30; Renner 120; Metz; and Derrick King paras 15–17.

19. Pointed out, among many others, by Derrick King, para. 1: 'It therefore seems that the idea of "free will," or freedom more generally, functions as nothing more than an ideological justification for the punishment doled out to the film's characters; it is then precisely because they are ostensibly "free" that they can be brutally sacrificed to the Ancient Ones.' On the complicity rule, see also Mayo 249 and Sessarego.

20. Kooyman has pointed out the scene's significance to the idea of freedom in a pre-determined context (in this case, the culture of horror remakes that force filmmakers to service a prescribed number of formulas): 'he is a slave to the materials and formulas he is assigned' (111). On the formulaic character of horror in this context, see also Blouin, 'Growing Global Darkness' 84.

21. This is very close to the interpretation of the film offered by Derrick King, who has read the film and particularly its ending slightly less philosophically and slightly more politically as a utopia that imagines a world beyond capitalist commodification.

22. Lockett 134.

23. McDonald para. 6.

24. Derrick King para. 24.

25. Derrick King para. 20.

26. The most spiteful of these are probably the IMDb reviews of the *Violator* group described by Lipsett, along with the anonymous review of *The Cabin in the Woods* script in *Scriptshadow*.

Chapter 4: Alignment v. Allegiance: How We See

One of the questions most frequently asked about *The Cabin in the Woods*, a film that shows us decent, funny and smart characters first being turned into clichés and then torn to shreds because that's all they are, is simply this: do we care? A surprising number of critics and reviewers have declared that we don't. If, as Stevens has claimed, 'these five are less characters than game pieces' who only 'exist so that the script can move them,' viewer devastation at their deaths will be muted.[1] The assumption here is that *Cabin* not so much critiques as mimics the horror genre's portrayal of victims, which is usually so deliberately inept, callous or contemptuous that identification with the victim is not an option. Does the Dumb Blonde who runs upstairs when she should have run outside garner the viewer's sympathy or scorn? Contempt for the victim is so pervasive in horror as to be an assumed viewer position, parodied, for example, in the horror-film spoof *Scary Movie* (2000), in which the victim, tearing out of the house, is confronted with two road signs: 'Safety' with an arrow pointing to the left, and 'Death' with an arrow pointing to the right. After a bit of dithering, she chooses—to nobody's surprise—'Death.'[2]

Whedon has vociferously objected to the genre's treatment of victims as 'just fodder' and its unrelenting focus on the villain 'because that's the action figure, and then we'll throw some expendable teenagers at them, and they get more and more expendable and more love is put into the instruments of torture…'[3] That Whedon made these comments in the context of his and Goddard's conceptualisation of *Cabin*'s teens indicates that they were intended to be more than expendable. They were meant to be characters with whom identification is not only possible but invited, and whose dreadful deaths might move us closer to tears than cheers. This bid for audience sympathy, at least according to the group of critics cited above, crashed like a motorbike against an invisible barrier. According to Cynthia Fuchs, describing her own response, 'you want the kid(s) to survive but also you don't, because you're in place to jump at startling-yet-unsurprising noises and faux scares and feel repulsed/titillated by bloody squishy effects, to worry at the point-of-view frame observing the girl undress and watch the victim scream and blubber as he or she is dragged away from the camera.'[4] In brief: same bloody squishy effects, same expendable teenagers, and you really couldn't care less.

Another camp of commentators have claimed that on the contrary, we care very much, and not only about the victims but also about their killers. The idea was first floated by Goddard and Whedon in their discussion of the scene in which the teens desperately try to escape through the tunnel—at this point still intact due to the Demolition Department's incompetence—and Sitterson equally desperately races to the bypass panel to fix the snafu. 'This,' Whedon and Goddard claim, 'is the film in a nutshell. You are rooting for both of them. You are absolutely desperate that they get through that tunnel and you are desperate that Sitterson gets his job done. ... In the end, if you look at this movie, both sides are right. ... They believe what they believe for a reason. And that reason is not ridiculous.'[5] This, in obvious contrast to the idea of audience aloofness, not only suggests strong identification, but in fact identification with opposing characters and the capacity to relate simultaneously to two incompatible desires, knowing that one of them will be disappointed. While the film-makers' comment implies simultaneity, most critics have translated this into a scenario of divided loyalties in which audiences sympathise and identify with different characters at different moments. As McDonald has put it, 'we become the unknowing sacrificial victims (sometimes), and we are the cold-hearted guardians of society (sometimes).'[6]

A third and final cluster of critics has answered the identification question in a slightly more complicated fashion: we'd like to care but can't because *Cabin*'s double life as horror and meta-horror forbids it. Far 'too often,' this school of thought claims, 'Whedon and Goddard want it both ways, trying to make the audience have a genuine reaction while at the same time never letting go of the self-conscious acknowledgment of what they are doing and the way they are leading the audience to that response.'[7] This third take on audience identification adapts the Brechtian idea that you can't be emotionally involved and analytically distant at the same time, and further assumes that *Cabin*'s narrative is essentially crushed by the weight of its meta-text:

> The process in this case unfolds broadly speaking as follows: the intertextual clues permit genre connoisseurs to experience themselves as pop-culturally savvy subjects

who partake in knowledge and expertise. On this level, which dominates the first two acts, a cognitive pleasure is evoked that can be described as enjoyment of one's own cleverness. Films in which ostentatious intertextuality dominates generally are less effective in provoking affect than those that try to give the viewer the illusion of a physical and affect-intensive involvement that is as immediate as possible. Intertextuality makes the latter more difficult since it always also insists that one is watching a film at this very moment and nothing else.[8]

Moldenhauer, the author of this passage, views *Cabin*'s offer to audiences as a world of eithers and ors: 'Intertextuality / The body in pain; Ironic distance / Immediacy; Genre expertise / Affective mimesis.'[9] If there is no path leading from one to the other, then viewers must either ignore *Cabin*'s meta-level to experience it as a horror film, or accept that their appreciation of *Cabin* as a meta-film renders them incapable of identification on the narrative level. The tunnel connecting emotional and analytic responses has, apparently, collapsed. Critics who pose this contrast tend to conclude that *Cabin* fails both at compassion and cognition, as a film and a meta-film, since 'a film created simply for the sake of regarding its own genre smarts is a hollow vessel. Without a human, emotional component, there actually isn't much to spoil.'[10] Indeed, the fiercest accusation that has been lobbed at *Cabin* is that it fails to make audiences care about its characters while attacking a horror tradition infamous for doing exactly the same thing.[11]

All three critical camps, what we might call the Carers, the Don't-Carers and the Can't-Carers, have zeroed in on one main idea: audience identification. The question when, how, why, and with whom we identify (or whether we do it at all) is the eye of the critical storm around *Cabin*, and perhaps rightly so, given that Whedon and Goddard considered the same question 'the film in a nutshell.' But is it true, as has so often been claimed, that Goddard and Whedon 'can't have it both ways,' which means essentially that the audience can't either? Assuming the incompatibility of empathetic and intellectual responses in real life would instantly mire us in nonsensical notions and dull every ethical sense we have. If a husband rationally accepts that his wife can't be saved and permits doctors to take her off life-support, does that mean that he no longer mourns for her and is thus undeserving of our sympathy? Any question that leads to an unbridgeable divide between affect and judgement is posed incorrectly. The real question, then, is why *Cabin* 'can't have it both ways,' why horror audiences shouldn't either, and whether the idea that we can't may not actually be the main problem here, for it forces us into another puppets' choice. Either we identify or we analyse. Either we see *Cabin* as a horror film or as meta-commentary on the genre. Either we sacrifice empathy—that part of us that recognises when innocents are savaged and responds with emotion—or awareness—that part of us that gleefully catalogues the monsters, giggles when conventions are capsized, and eventually questions our own role in all this.

Where we, the audience, are in all this is seen as central to the question of identification, and, of course, vice versa. If Goddard and Whedon are right in saying that we are perfectly capable of identifying both with the teens' desire to escape and Sitterson's attempts to prevent their escape, the position from which we identify is not fixed. Levy is half-way there when he claims that 'We're forced, finally, to ask whether we're more like the luckless souls trapped in "The Cabin in the Woods" or the ironic sadists who selfishly concoct such dooms.'[12] As an initial question, this will serve; as a 'finally,' it merely lands us in yet another 'either v. or.' McDonald comes closer when he proposes that 'We, along with the characters in the movie, take up multiple roles with regards to the three basic roles of "victim" (the sacrificial scapegoat), "community" (the unanimous society warding off violence through sacrificial rites) and "gods" (the supposed recipients and authenticators of the sacrifice).'[13] At first reading, this too makes sense: where on the sliding scale from victims to gods we see ourselves at any moment in the film will determine whether we respond with affect or intellect. Yet even this slightly more complex identification model still does not allow us to 'have it both ways'; it still assigns streamlined responses to each audience persona, as modelled by McDonald:

> As it shifts the roles of victim from the young adults to the Men Behind the Scenes [MBS], the audience becomes aware that it has something at stake in this violence. [...] Of course, if the audience identifies itself with the desire to sacrifice the young adults for the greater good (like the MBS), then it also must accept responsibility for the sacrificial violence which purportedly has served to maintain all the societies

throughout the film's world. Moreover, [...] the audience might very well be expected to identify with the deities destined to receive the sacrifice. After all, it is the audience, not the Gods, that is the driving force behind the horror genre; viewers made all this violence necessary through the price of admission.[14]

This describes an almost mathematically ordered universe of audience identification and the responses it occasions. If we identify with victims, we sympathise with their suffering; if we identify with the MBS, we accept responsibility for inflicting it; if we identify with the Gods, we recognise ourselves as its cause. Audience responses are reduced to the choice between compassion and cognition, governed by identification either way, and—although elicited by mimetic artforms—presumed to be considerably less complex than any response to real-life events. Where in all these shifting roles and their inflexible identification patterns is the *synchronicity* assumed by Whedon and Goddard, the audience's ability to root, simultaneously and hopelessly, for incompatible outcomes? Where is the horror viewer's ability to 'have it both ways,' to respond rationally and analytically while tossed about in a maelstrom of emotions, as a husband contemplating the off switch on his wife's respirator might?

So far, this question has not come up in *Cabin*-criticism, not even in response to Goddard and Whedon's suggestive nutshell-remark. Instead, either v. or reigns supreme. At this point, we might consider a return to Square One, for if the answer always boils down to an either/or alternative, we may be asking the wrong question. In other words: if the puppet's choice between affect and analysis is manacled to identification, the idea of identification itself may be unsound.

Some thinkers have, in fact, proposed precisely that. Murray Smith, for instance, has built an entire theory of how we relate to film characters on two objections to what he calls the 'folk theory' of identification. His first objection is to the idea that identification assumes two static entities—spectator and character—and two static alternatives: either we identify or we don't.[15] His second objection addresses 'the *paradox of fiction* (the idea that in responding to fictions we behave at once as if we know, and as if we do not know, that we are perceiving a mere fiction), and the *reason–emotion antinomy* (the idea that emotion and reason are at odds with one another).'[16] How this is relevant to *Cabin* should be instantly obvious. Identification, by far the most prominent topic in *Cabin* literature, suffers from all three—the folk theory of static alternatives; the Brechtian reason–emotion antinomy; and an inability to transcend the paradox of fiction. In *Cabin*'s case, that paradox is exacerbated by the film's double life as meta-horror (which entices viewers to behave as if they know that they're looking at fiction) and narrative horror (where they're encouraged to behave as if they don't know).

Smith identifies character structure as the major way in which a narrative text engages its audience, but considers this a complicated process hopelessly short-changed by the term 'identification.' He proposes replacing the concept with a more differentiated 'structure of sympathy' whose cornerstones he terms 'alignment' and 'allegiance.' Alignment describes the manner in which a film allows us access to the characters' actions, thoughts and feelings; allegiance the way in which a film marshals audience sympathy or antipathy on a character's behalf.[17] Smith's system instantly does away with all sorts of wrong-headed notions: that 'identification' forces the viewer to accommodate to prevailing ideology; that it is difficult for a film to 'align' us with an unsympathetic character (or indeed to secure our allegiance to such a person); that camera angles or point-of-view shots necessarily entail either alignment or allegiance (let alone 'identification'); that sight can be equated with subjectivity; and that ideological judgements can be equated with morality.[18] Smith's distinction between alignment and allegiance allows us to differentiate between a purely cognitive audience response (alignment) and one that may also be emotional (allegiance), without assuming that cognition automatically torpedoes compassion.[19] Perhaps Smith's greatest achievement

> is not to assume an all-powerful text and a prostrate spectator, but a spectator who responds to the text with a knowledge of all the relevant conventions that the text draws upon for the particular effect in question. Neither does this assume that this is all that a spectator may do—simply that the text is designed to elicit this response from an appropriately knowledgeable spectator.[20]

This, it seems to me, comes quite a bit closer to the more independent and also more complex range of possible audience responses imagined by Whedon and

Goddard. Where Smith goes beyond even them is in presuming a potentially considerable gulf between a film's offer to audiences—of either alignment or allegiance—and what audiences then do with that offer. Drawing on Noël Carroll's ideas on 'assimilation' and a-central imagining (the proposition that audiences respond to emotional states on the screen with a suitable but different emotion) and quite possibly also on Stuart Hall's taxonomy of the dominant, oppositional and negotiating reader, Smith concludes that the idea of 'identification' vastly overrates a film's control over audience response.[21] As a result, he aims to shift the entire discussion away from the quagmire of how we see and back to the firmer ground of how fictional films *invite* us to see.

Another thinker who can help us reconsider identification is the comic artist Scott McCloud, who, writing a year before Smith, grappled with it in comics in a way that seems highly applicable to narrative film. Similar to Genette, who has claimed that identification with a cinematic protagonist relies on a 'systematic restriction of information,'[22] McCloud draws a direct link between reader identification and a process of character abstraction in which 'we're not so much *eliminating* details as we are *focusing* on *specific details*. By *stripping down* an image to its essential "*meaning*," an artist can *amplify* that meaning in a way that realistic art *can't*.'[23] What film scholars have called 'identification' is achieved through what McCloud has termed 'amplification through simplification.' The simpler and more cartoonish the image of a person, the more we tend to fill in the blanks with aspects of ourselves; the more specific the person drawn, the less we are able to do this. 'Thus, when you look at a photo or realistic drawing of a face—you see it as the face of *another*. But when you enter the world of the *cartoon*—you see *yourself*.'[24] Theoretically, then, we should identify most strongly with the most generic cartoon drawing of a human face: a circle with two dots and a line inside it.

According to McCloud, though, we don't so much 'identify' as experience a 'sense of general placement' that allows us to inject ourselves into scenarios experienced by a fictional protagonist. The more generic (cartoonish) the character, the more readily we do this (because it could be anyone). But also: the more generic (cartoonish) the character, the less it resembles a human being—this is true in both the world of comics and in that of horror. All this directly contradicts the 'folk theory,' which assumes that identification is most readily bestowed upon the most fascinating, appealing and recognisably human protagonist at hand. But it would certainly come closer than the identification model to explaining what is otherwise difficult to rationalise: that a horror audience is more likely to respond to screen savagery with cheers for the baddie than with tears for the victim.

To illustrate how we might approach *Cabin*'s characters differently than through the monocle of 'identification,' I would like to focus on one compendium of scenes in which a complex character is simplified in order to amplify her assigned role, and ask what parts alignment and allegiance play in these cinematic moments. The scenes I have in mind could be assembled under the heading 'The Whorification of Jules.' They are situated in a context of scenes showing her to be something *other* than the Whore. At first appearance she is characterised as a loyal friend trying to help Dana past the misery of a recent breakup and as an equal partner to Curt, who has established himself as a sound and strategic thinker in his conversation with Dana and with whom Jules engages in quick-witted repartee that shows her ability to give as good as she gets. In the gas station scene, she is singled out for particular abuse by Mordecai, who spits tobacco across her path, yells an insult at her and then calls her a 'whore.' To the shouted insult she responds by shrinking in fear against Curt; to the 'whore' moniker she responds with outrage. Significantly, it is not only Curt who rises to her defence: Marty's wonderfully sassy civil-war dig needs no further justification than 'You were rude to my friend,' and all three men in the group both defend her verbally and insert themselves physically between Jules and Mordecai (fig. 13). Clearly, the audience is led to think, Jules must have done something right to inspire such loyalty, not only from her boyfriend but from everyone in the group. In fact, our 'sense of general placement' allows us to envision ourselves in the situation and conclude—without really 'identifying' with anyone on screen—that Jules has done nothing to provoke this abuse and that she deserves both the group's protection and the friendship it expresses.

Figure 13. Jules, her attacker and her protectors

All of this—the group's (and the audience's) admiration for Jules's kindness, wit and *joie de vivre* in the first scene; the group's (and the audience's) protective instincts towards her at the gas station—is unceremoniously erased by the Whorification of Jules. This process works precisely as described by McCloud, by amplification through simplification. To say that the stock horror type (the Whore) is a simplification of Jules's original character is narratively true, but it says nothing about the cinematographic means that effect her transformation from character to cliché. In fact, it is less the narrative than the camera that simplifies Jules, and it does so by turning her into body parts (to cite McCloud again: 'we're not so much *eliminating* details as we are *focusing* on *specific details*'). Having accepted Marty's dare to make out with the wolf, Jules takes a big swallow from her tankard of beer—what a lush, is the insinuation to the audience—and vaults over the sofa to land with cat-like grace on both feet. A slow pan up her lower body ensues as she sashays towards her target, the camera focusing sequentially on her feet and calves, knees and thighs, thighs and a bottom barely covered by her skimpy shorts (figs 14–16), and finally her swaying back. The climax of the scene, pun most definitely intended, is a close-up kiss of the wolf's head involving tongue on both sides (fig. 17).

Figures 14–16. Pieces of Jules

Figure 17. Focusing on the details: tongues

In a parallel scene showing Jules dancing suggestively in front of the fireplace, with her friends looking on as if they did not recognise this person, we do get a whole body-shot, but we are still focusing on the details. This time it is not a close-up but camera positioning that supplies the focus; the camera's gaze, positioned too low to mimic an observer sitting on the couch, implies a fictional viewer lying on the floor, in prime position to look up Jules's shorts in hopes of catching a glimpse of her butt cheeks (fig. 18). That Jules's dissection is again the point is corroborated by dialogue—Curt asking Marty whether he wouldn't want 'a piece of that,' and Marty, still traumatised by Patience Buckner's 'My right arm is hacked off and et,' begging off: 'Can we not talk about people in pieces anymore tonight?' Following this, we will be treated to more pieces of Jules: her bare breasts, eagerly anticipated Downstairs, and finally her decapitated head, flung contemptuously at Dana who catches it by shock reflex. The dissection and finally dismemberment of Jules proceeds in a systematic and deliberate fashion, from feet, ankles, calves and thighs to butt, breasts and head: we're moving up until we are literally looking at the last piece of what used to be a whole character (fig. 19).

Figure 18. Focusing on the details: butt

Figure 19. Dana looks at the last piece of Jules

Amplification through simplification works in a literal manner on Jules, who is simplified to serve as the film's 'whore' by the relentless amplification of her body parts. Obviously, this has nothing to do with traditional 'identification'; as a type, Jules is no longer eligible. McCloud's idea that we respond to simplification with a greater sense of placement may get us a bit further, for this implies the genre familiarity that Moldenhauer has touched upon. We, seasoned horror viewers that we are, observe the Whore's swaying hips, her jutting butt, her bare breasts, and we know this means that pretty soon, her head will come off. Our sense of placement assures us of where we are and what will happen next, whereas the more complex Jules of the first scene might have presented us with any number of unpredictable scenarios. This, perhaps, goes some way towards explaining McCloud's apparently paradoxical assertion that the more simplified and generic an entity is, the more we 'identify.' As complex characters, before their simplification to the stock types of horror, the five teens correspond to 'a photo or realistic drawing of a face' which we are likely to perceive 'as the face of *another*.' Once we enter the world of horror, or in McCloud's words 'the world of the *cartoon*,' we may be able to insert ourselves—not in the sense of 'identification' but in the sense of *recognition*. We assume a secure position vis-à-vis the fictional world; we know what kind of a world it is; we recognise its characters as game pieces; and we can predict the outcome. Sense of placement and recognition are both a far cry from the traditional idea of identification. We cannot 'identify' with the Whore, but certainly, if we have ever experienced helpless rage, we recognise it when we see the stock characters of horror bash against their cages. Unlike 'identification,' sense of placement and recognition are embedded in situations, not characters.

The dances-with-wolf scene does raise the question why the camera (Goddard's camera) is playing the Downstairs game. Does this mean that critics were right to accuse *Cabin* of callousness towards its characters and hypocrisy for criticising other horror films for the same sin? To an audience seeking to 'identify,' it would mean precisely that. Yet if we approach Jules's dissection through the model proposed by Smith, we might ask instead why our view of Jules is being aligned with that of the showrunners Downstairs, and what this does to our allegiance to her in earlier scenes. In fact, the Jules-scenes are a good illustration of the relationship between alignment and allegiance described by Smith, namely that they are distinct and able to function independently. The sequence progresses from a scenario where alignment and allegiance harmonise to one where they are diametrically opposed. In the gas station scene, alignment matches allegiance. Our sense of placement is in synch with the group protecting Jules from attack; we *want* to be part of the little protective circle that separates Mordecai from Jules. In the dances-with-wolf scene, alignment and allegiance are at odds, for a character that commanded our allegiance only a few short scenes earlier is now being dissected and simplified. The dialogue ('C'mon, like you wouldn't want a piece of that' / 'Can we not talk about people in pieces anymore') tells us exactly where this is headed: into a set-up that offers us the usual dirty deal of horror—sex and violence—and that will end with the second punishing the first. The scene is, essentially, a misalignment of the audience, not for the purpose of replacing Jules's character with a type and depriving her of the audience's allegiance, but for the purpose of begging the question: Can allegiance be broken by alignment? We know from earlier scenes that Jules is anything but a 'whore,' but the camera in her dance scenes says she is. Are we now fully aligned with seeing Jules as no more than a bunch of disconnected body parts? Or does our allegiance to Jules, so pervasive at the gas station, still hold? And if not, what would this indicate about our ethical and empathetic abilities as viewers?

Cabin's teens can certainly be read as predictable, flat, boring, expendable victims that nobody really cares about; too many critics have done it to deny that the possibility exists. Others, however, have responded to the slaughter of innocents with extraordinary levels of allegiance, and the more the characters are flattened to justify the butchery, the louder the clamour of indignation pointing out that they were unjustly and brutally stripped not only of their diegetic existence but also of a depth that would have entitled them to audience sympathies. This is, perhaps, why Jules, the first to die and the one who is simplified most egregiously, has also attracted the greatest degree of allegiance-fuelled outrage. 'Only Jules has a long, drawn out, humiliating, terrifying death scene in which she is stripped of not only her clothing but also her dignity,' laments Sessarego, and elaborates:

> Dana and Marty could be said to triumph, because they die on their own terms. Jules doesn't get to triumph. Her death doesn't lead to any victory or discovery. Her death is not avenged [...]. The most horrifying thing isn't that Jules isn't really The Whore (she's too nice, too smart, and too monogamous to fit the role as it usually plays out in slasher movies). Worse is the suggestion that it's okay to kill Jules as long as she can be thought of as The Whore. What if Jules really did like doing sexy dances? What if she and Curt were in an open relationship and she slept with a different person every night of the week? Would this magically make it acceptable for a zombie to cut off her head with a saw?[25]

Clearly, the attitude described in this passage goes well beyond 'identification,' a stance that would not only lead us back to the all-powerful film and the prostate viewer, but also presumably end with the film. The sentiment expressed here does not. Fuelled within the film by what Smith has called 'allegiance,' it endures beyond it by what

McCloud has termed a 'sense of placement.' It recognises not the character as 'me' (as identification would) but the *situation* as one that might be inflicted on any woman, as a sense of placement does.

Finally, I would like to return for a moment to Smith's distinction between alignment and allegiance and ask why *Cabin*, at least in the Jules-sequence, expresses alignment almost exclusively through images (for example the slow pan up her body in the dance scenes) and allegiance almost exclusively through words (for example Marty's verbal sparring with Mordecai). McCloud, whose work as a comic artist is governed by the nexus of word and image, has described the relationship as follows:

> Pictures are **received** information. [...] Writing is **perceived** information. [...] When pictures are more abstracted from "reality," they require greater levels of *perception*, **more like words**. When words are bolder, more direct, they require *lower* levels of perception and are perceived *faster*, **more like pictures**. Our need for a unified **language** [...] sends us toward the center where words and pictures are like two sides of *one coin*! But our need for **sophistication** [...] seems to lead us *outward*, where words and pictures are most *separate*. [...] Can they be reconciled?[26]

The world of images, then, fulfils different needs than the world of words, and it is uncertain whether the two can be reconciled. *The Cabin in the Woods* can be seen as a precise reproduction of both the struggle and the final question. Its doppelganger-status as a horror film and a meta-commentary on the genre is not, as some reviewers have claimed, a design flaw ('Two distinct kinds of movie are being yoked, by violence, together'[27]) but a structure deliberately adopted to confront audiences with a question rarely asked of horror viewers: how we see. Are we receivers of images or perceivers of words? When the cinematography directly contradicts our perception of a character established by narrative, which do we believe? Which will figure more strongly in our memory of Jules: Marty's witty defence of her at the gas station and her worthiness of it, or ogling her 'boobies'?

Much like McCloud sees his readers, Goddard's film implies an audience that is both a receiver (of pictures) and a perceiver (of words), beset by the need for both a unified language and sophistication, and uncertain whether these needs can be reconciled. For the first half of the film, *Cabin* portrays a split not only between Upstairs and

Downstairs, but also between words and pictures, with images very often conflicting directly with narrative, as we have seen in the Jules-sequence. The second half of the film represents both a transition from words to pictures and a sequential simplification of images. The fully rounded characters of the film's first scene are, in the last, simplified into primitive cave drawings on a temple wall, mere outlines filled not with content but with blood. Similarly, the horrors that might befall humanity are deprived of a narrative space where they might be defanged by dialogue, exchange, compassion, solidarity, humour or analysis. Instead, each is represented as an image of a monster imprisoned in a cage the way a picture is contained by a frame (fig. 20). Once Marty and Dana hit the 'Purge All' button, the frames separating individual horrors are discarded; the picture gallery merges into a single image that we might suspect is Whedon and Goddard's shorthand for torture-porn horror (fig. 21).

Figure 20. Cabin's *image gallery of horrors*

As a horror flick, *Cabin* showcases the trauma inherent in the descent from word to image; as a meta-horror film, *Cabin* illustrates what may happen to viewers when the image overwhelms the word, when pictures trump narrative, when we are too busy *receiving* to bother *perceiving* anymore. Traditional horror, the film proclaims, will always try to drown perception in received images; it will always try to stunt our capacity for compassion, our cognitive abilities and our ethical sense. What horror does to its characters—flattening them into types—is, at the end of the day, no more than an image of what it might do to its viewers. That giant evil hand smashing the world flat at the end of the film is actually coming for *you*.

Figure 21. The single image

But you are not defenceless; far from it. As Smith has said, there isn't only the choice between identification and alienation.[28] There are also cognition and compassion, perceptiveness and words. There is also, as McCloud has said, a sense of placement that enables you to recognise when a character is unfairly simplified and then railroaded for it. And perhaps that same sense will be there to tell you that your own character will be diminished if you can be made to relinquish your allegiance to someone because a few images have fooled you into believing that she's no more than a 'whore.'

Notes

1. Stevens in her review of the film in *Slate*; agreeing with her are Debruge; Whitty; Levy; McLevy and James; Olsen; Fuchs; Giannini, 'Charybdis'; and Sterba 162–3.
2. To clarify: my claim here is not that horror provides no other 'pleasures' than seeing victims dispatched; that horror has more on offer, including sophisticated pleasures linked to intertextuality and self-awareness, has been amply shown by Philip Brophy and Brigid Cherry. Equally obviously, horror's contempt for victims is a general trend rather than an inevitability: although they are a minority, counter-examples of sympathetic and beloved characters being dispatched in horror films can easily be found. A further objection that could be made here is that the villain/victim dichotomy is more prominent in horror's subgenre, the slasher film, and that *Cabin* evokes the slasher film (monsters in elevators; weird objects in basements) more obviously than it does horror entire (see, for example, Dana Stevens). To this I would answer that Goddard and Whedon (the latter called *Cabin* his 'loving hate-letter to *horror*') clearly meant to cast their net more widely: their film's

indictment for the crime of typecasting characters to discourage affective responses to their slaughter targets the genre at large. Much like horror, slasher films, too, from *Halloween* to *Scream*, have played with the victim/villain relationship and presumed audience views of both, which indicates both that the slasher (and horror) film's relationship with its characters is by no means unsophisticated *and* that the genre perceives contempt for the victim as a general trend. For the victim/villain dichotomy and the pleasure offers in slasher films specifically, see Clayton; Pheasant-Kelly; and Petridis.

3. Whedon and Goddard, *The Cabin in the Woods: The Official Visual Companion* 150. Whedon is not alone in surmising that horror's unremitting focus on the cult villain and contempt for the victim has cost the genre audience allegiance in the past: 'After years of raking in the bloodstained bucks off the corpses of fictional dead teenagers, the sun finally seemed to be setting on the slasher genre until the mid-90s rolled around to revivify its hulking corpse' (McGovern).

4. Fuchs in her review of the film in *PopMatters*.

5. Goddard and Whedon on the DVD commentary, as quoted by Kowalski, *Joss Whedon as Philosopher* 180. On this scene, see also Parrish para. 31.

6. McDonald para. 6; see also his paras 7 and 14; Kowalski; Moldenhauer, 'Somatische Empathie' 29; Parrish para. 31; Pascale 319–20; Richardson 50; Venezia 412 and 414; and Sessarego.

7. Olsen in *Village Voice*.

8. Moldenhauer, 'Somatische Empathie' 28–9, my translation of 'Dieser Verlauf sieht in diesem Falle im Groben aus wie folgt: Die intertextuellen Verweise erlauben es dem Genrekenner, sich als popkulturell versiertes Subjekt zu erleben, das Teil an einem Expertenwissen hat. Auf dieser, die ersten beiden Akte dominierenden Ebene wird ein vor allem kognitives Vergnügen evoziert, das sich als Freude an der eigenen Cleverness fassen lässt. Filme, in denen ostentative Intertextualität dominiert, wirken affektiv gemeinhin weniger intensiv als solche, die darauf zielen, dem Zuschauer die Illusion einer möglichst unmittelbaren körperlichen und affektintensiven Involvierung zu verschaffen. Intertextualität erschwert Letztere, da sie immer auch darauf insistiert, dass man just in diesem Moment einen Film und nichts anderes sieht.'

9. Moldenhauer, 'Somatische Empathie,' 29: 'Intertextualität / Körper im Schmerz; Ironische Distanz / Unmittelbarkeit; Genrewissen / Affektive Mimesis.'

10. Olsen; see also Ryan J. Parker, who claims, echoing Noël Carroll's dichotomy of horror and humour, that comedy on the film's meta-level 'unsettles the horror and complicates our engagement with it' (207). Kristopher Karl Woofter has similarly written extensively, and critically, on the film's 'diminishment of affect for the sake of crucial distance' (273–8, the quotation on 273).

11. For example in Sterba 162: 'The idea of making these characters people, in whom we take general interest, is a good instinct, but it clashes a bit with another of the filmmakers' goals—that of laying bare the tired tropes of contemporary horror film. By playing on the typical character stereotypes, "Whedard" risks falling right back into the same stale stories being decried and reducing viewer interest in the characters. [...] Unfortunately, this sounds a bit like the torture porn condemned by Whedon in his interviews.'
12. Levy in the *Oregonian*; similarly Venezia, who claims that 'spectatorial perspective and sympathy shift back and forth' (412).
13. McDonald para. 7.
14. McDonald para. 14; the same conclusion has been reached by others (for example, Richardson 50).
15. Smith 3.
16. Smith 3 (emphases original).
17. Smith 7.
18. Smith 7, 10, 84, 157.
19. Smith 187.
20. Smith 64.
21. Smith 228.
22. See Genette; the citation from his work in Smith 83.
23. McCloud 30 (all emphases original).
24. McCloud 36 (emphases original).
25. Sessarego (unpag.).
26. McCloud 49 (all emphases original).
27. A. O. Scott in *The New York Times*.
28. Smith 6.

Chapter 5: Guilt v. Fear: Why We Look

> *Why do we crave horror movies?*
> *Stephen King*[1]

> *Why do we need horror stories? And I don't mean enjoy, I mean NEED. We revel in them. And maybe that's a response to the darkness of the world (or an inoculation against it) or maybe it really is why we need to be gotten rid of.*
> *Joss Whedon*[2]

The question has confounded not only two of the most acclaimed writers in the field, but also virtually everyone who has written about it.[3] It is, of course, unanswerable; there is no conceivable 'because' that could stand up to this prodigiously despairing 'why.' Our options in addressing it are thus limited. So far we seem to have exercised three: we have, as the Magic 8 Ball would have us do, asked again later, with increasing frequency, urgency and evocative emphasis on the *why* ('why we need to return to these sorts of films, why we love to laugh and jump, why we hunger for carnage and thirst for blood'[4]). We have also offered shoddy answers or, as Whedon did, left the question open. And yet an attempt to respond has to be made because the why-question, while consistently raised *by* horror, is not *about* horror but instead one of the most urgent inquiries that can be made about human nature. Seen 'from this perspective,' writes Canavan, 'horror becomes the most serious thing there could be: horror bespeaks an existential-theological crisis about the soul of humanity that cries desperately out for some explanation, if not a solution.'[5] This would make horror one of the most profoundly philosophical genres in the realm of fiction, and engaging the why-question an ethical obligation for everyone involved with it.

Why *do* we look? Why do audiences regularly, voluntarily, even eagerly expose themselves to something that is so manifestly unpleasant? Let us start with one of the sloppy answers we have so far: that horror is all about fear, and that we watch it because we enjoy experiencing a good scare from a position of safety. If 'horror' as an emotion is defined as 'what we feel when anything frightens us or promotes fear or terror,'[6] it seems to follow that horror as a genre is all about *Creating and Marketing Fear*.[7] Fear, in this thinking, becomes not merely the genre's main but actually its sole prerequisite: 'If it is the movie's aim to terrify, horrify or frighten, it qualifies as a horror production.'[8] Yet in assuming that 'The horror film has the intent to horrify,'[9] we confuse horror as an *experience* with horror as a *genre*. Once we have muddied the waters in this fashion, the basic formula—horror (the emotion) = fear; ergo horror (film) *evokes* fear—becomes difficult to question.

But perhaps we should. If H. P. Lovecraft, undeniably the godfather of horror, was right in saying that 'the oldest and strongest kind of fear is fear of the unknown,'[10] it is difficult to imagine a genre *less* qualified to evoke fear than horror. Horror films do not deal with the unknown. On the contrary, they practically epitomise predictability, and their most basic building blocks, mandated by the time-honoured rule that horror's victims must be complicit in their demise, are repetition and exacerbation. Someone gets into trouble and does not back off. He then gets into worse trouble, but fails to back off. He then gets into catastrophic trouble, and far from backing off, he walks blithely on, straight into apocalyptic trouble. At this point, more often than not, his head comes off.

Are we scared yet?

Remember Kirk in *The Texas Chain Saw Massacre*? Why, if he's already weirded out by the heads of freshly dead animals mounted on the wall and the sounds of pigs screaming, does he walk up to Leatherface's metal door? Remember Darry in *Jeepers Creepers*? If he already strongly suspects that the Creeper has thrown a bloody corpse down the pipe, why does he have to go look instead of driving off at top speed and calling the cops? The point about horror and fear, and the main reason why fear is not the principal driver of horror films, is this: nobody is ever scared *enough*. This is, of course, why the characters of horror get into ever-greater trouble. But it also applies to the viewer. Nothing shows this more clearly than the jump scare, a ubiquitous horror feature that really isn't much more than a reminder to the audience to be scared. The implication seems to be that the viewer actually *isn't* scared, or rather, much like horror's characters, not scared enough, and certainly also not scared for long enough. Otherwise, why all the jump cuts, fright music and slamming doors? Does the need to shock the audience into an extra-terrifying split second not imply that fear is, by definition, fleeting? Does it not imply that outside of that brief adrenalin injection or sometimes just sheer noise—bang, bang, you're deaf—the horror film isn't actually all that frightening? Screaming, vomiting, fainting, edge-of-the-seat perching and nail biting can only be kept up for so long. Fear simply doesn't have enough of a shelf life to serve as the main driver of a horror film, at least not one that aims for an effect lasting beyond the time it takes to screen.

A typical horror film is not about fear but familiarity. It gets the same kind of character into the same kind of trouble, over and over again. We *know* that Kirk will not stick with opening the door and hello-ing down the hallway, but go into the house. We *know* that Darry will lean so far down the pipe that he'll eventually fall in. We know that evil can be vanquished only provisionally, that our satisfaction in seeing the Creeper run over, Michael Myers burnt to a crisp, or Chucky melted into a puddle of plastic is temporary. We know they will all be back in the sequel.[11] We know these things whether we have seen the film or not. Horror reliably presents us with the worst-case scenario. Is it possible to fear it if we know it's coming, if we expect it, even rely on it?

While *Cabin*-critics have not managed to agree on much, one of two points of near-universal accord is that the film is just not scary.[12] Most have taken this as evidence that *Cabin* is too concerned with its geeky meta-persona to succeed as a horror film, which won't get a critical stamp of approval unless it scares your socks off. To this common condemnation I would like to offer an alternative: that *Cabin* is after something other than fear; that it shares this goal with its genre; and that it is this—more than its snarky commentary and genre-jokes—that makes *Cabin* eligible for consideration as horror's belated prototype.

Before we get to the 'something other,' though, let us briefly test the fear-theory on *Cabin*. If, as I have argued in the previous chapter, the Brechtian model that precludes allegiance with a character does not sit easily with the film, perhaps the fear-theory will hold more water. After all, it was originally proposed by Aristotle, the very thinker whose ideas Brecht's theory aimed to debunk.[13] In Aristotle's model, tragedy seeks to evoke fear and pity in the audience, with the ultimate aim of affecting a 'purification' of these emotions (catharsis). Fear and pity function as the forebears of what we might call 'identification' in the sense that like identification, they target character and audience simultaneously: you experience pity with a character's fate only because you fear that the same might happen to you.[14] And yet, Aristotle's paradigm maps as badly onto *Cabin* as Brecht's anti-Aristotelian model does. In fact, *Cabin* seems to toy rather flippantly with Aristotle's terms, exposing them repeatedly as pale imitations of the real thing. Fear is a shadow of the genuine article in the gas station scene, palpably present but not remotely strong enough to convince the teens to turn back. The message to the viewer is the same as that of every jump scare or every gas station scene: nobody is ever scared enough. Pity comes in for an even worse drubbing as Hadley watches Dana, badly bruised from her battle with a Buckner, swim for her life. 'It's so strange,' he muses dreamily. 'I'm actually rooting for this girl. She's got so much heart. And you think of all the pain and the… Tequila is my *lady*! My *lady*!!' What briefly masqueraded as pity is actually no more than cheap sentimentality, forgotten as soon as booze arrives for the post-slaughter party. And could there be a more savage smack-down of catharsis than the Director's offer of 'purification' of fear and pity through self-sacrifice ('You can die with them. Or you can die for them'), skewered by Marty's derisive 'Gosh, they're both so enticing'? Unlike an Aristotelian tragedy, *Cabin* rejects the idea that the road to catharsis can be paved with human bodies, defines pity as phony, and proclaims that fear is beside the point.

What, then, *is* the point? To move towards it, we need to consider the second issue on which the film's critics have actually agreed: that *Cabin* aligns its audiences not with the film's victims but with its perpetrators—with the Evil Gods requiring the slaughter of teens, with the Downstairs personnel watching it on their screens, or both.[15] Sitterson and Hadley, the senior scenario engineers, are also commonly identified as stand-ins for the film's writing team, and with good reason, given that Whedon and Goddard owned up to the kinship in unambiguous terms: 'Anybody who thinks that Drew and I are not Hadley and Sitterson clearly never met us.'[16] To this act of identification, Whedon added a moral dimension in an interview that drew comparisons between *Cabin*'s senior showrunners and its writing team:

> I'm fine with that analogy. Here's my secret: I kill teenagers. I am the stuff in the basement. And this movie, and all these movies teach you, Don't go down in the basement. Because Drew and Joss are down there, having a meeting. We love horror. Clearly there's something wrong with us, and we celebrate that.[17]

Clearly, this being the case, there is also something wrong with the fear-theory of horror. Were fear the point of horror, its audiences would have to be aligned with those who have most reason to fear, the victims—just like the audience of an Aristotelian tragedy. Yet what is there to fear for an audience aligned with the architects of horror, the bureaucrats orchestrating a massacre or the Evil Gods baying for blood? *Cabin*'s critics, having agreed on two points—that it is not a scary film, and that its audiences are not aligned with the victims but the perps—have failed to draw the logical conclusion strongly suggested by both insights:[18] that *Cabin* is not concerned with fear but with guilt. Those who have faulted the film for not being scary enough have missed its point. *Cabin* has no intention of taking its viewers on a scary ride. Instead, it aims to send them on a guilt trip.

Mesmerised by *Cabin*'s witty genre commentary, scholars have routinely mistaken it for the film's main event while *Cabin*'s creators have described it as no more than an aside. To them, the point was not, as scholars have guessed, to replace torture porn with 'aesthetically valuable horror films'[19] or to write a film featuring 'a new earnestness (as well as, not least, better jokes).'[20] 'This movie does comment on a horror movie,' Goddard said in an interview, 'but that wasn't our goal. We wanted to comment more on who we are and what part horror plays in us as people.'[21] The authors' focus, then, was not so much on what horror does to *us* but on the question what we do with *it*.

The scene that addresses the issue most directly is barely 90 seconds long, but it certainly leaves an impression. To Goddard, it was shorthand for the entire film; to the studio financing it, it was the only scene in *Cabin* deemed too horrible to show. Pascale describes the dramatic rescue of a sequence that came close to expiring on the cutting room floor:

> MGM wanted the filmmakers to cut a particular sequence from the movie: before Dana and Marty discover the truth about the secret facility, their tormentors believe that the latter has been killed, so they gather to celebrate the successful completion of the sacrifice. The studio had issues with the idea that Sitterson, Hadley, and their colleagues would throw a big, alcohol-fueled party as Dana continued to struggle against their monsters on the monitors around the room.

To Drew Goddard, that juxtaposition told the story of *The Cabin in the Woods*. [...] Joss, as Goddard's producer, went back and forth with MGM over the issue, until he conceded that it was a battle that they had lost. Sitting in the editing room, Goddard started to cry, because it was a battle that he didn't want to lose.

Joss stared at Goddard, then turned and picked up the phone to call the studio head. He simply told them that they were not cutting the sequence from the film. Goddard exhaled. 'Oh, thank God.'[22]

Why the studio objected so strenuously to this scene bears thinking about. Too brutal? Certainly not. The sequence features no decapitation, impalement, evisceration, cannibalism, dismemberment or immolation, all of which occur elsewhere in the film and were waved through by the censors. Because it implicates the filmmakers, producers or studio? Partly, perhaps. Some commentators have remarked on the accolades showered upon Hadley (Goddard/Whedon) at the party, due tribute for his (their) skill at serving up slaughter while adhering to the rules of the sacrifice scenario (horror genre) to the letter, Final Girl and all. 'It's masterful,' titter the fans surrounding Hadley. 'Classic dénouement. When the van hits the lake [...] I screamed. [...] Primal terror.'[23] Yet all the fawning notwithstanding, the actual 'dénouement' of this supposedly accomplished ritual (movie)—Dana being savaged on the screen as the party hits full swing—attracts only an audience of one: Truman, the squeamish security guard (fig. 22). Everyone else is busy munching, drinking, clinking bottles, dancing, buttering up slightly more powerful colleagues, being snubbed by more attractive colleagues (fig. 23) or worrying about being paid overtime (fig. 24). Dana, currently dying on the screen behind them—at their hands, no less—fails to register as a human being worth saving, even as a movie character worthy of allegiance, distanced as she is from the partygoers' view (and from ours) by the grainy monochrome screen showing her mauling (fig. 25). How sincere is acclaim for a movie if nobody's interested in watching the ending? Even Hadley, whose 'mastery' is being complimented, is bored with the 'classic' horror tropes he employs with such dexterity: 'I just think it would've been cooler with a merman.'

Figure 22. An audience of one: Truman watches the dénouement

Figure 23. 'It's funny that you like the ballet, because I happen to have two tickets…'

Figure 24. 'You know if we'll get the overtime bonus on this one?'

Figure 25. Grainy Dana

And yet the scene does not merely implicate the film's producers. Were this merely another genre-commentary scene, notwithstanding Goddard's assertion that genre commentary 'wasn't our goal,' it could have been cut and replaced with one of many others of its kind throughout the film. Certainly, it would not have merited either a protracted battle with the studio or directorial tears at the thought of losing it. The reason Goddard considered the party scene emblematic of the entire film is that it shows more clearly than any other 'what part horror plays in us as people.' What nastiness it features implicates not the genre but its audience. Every aspect of the sequence indicates this, from the relatable inanity of the party dialogue to the muting of Dana's suffering through dark, monochrome and grainy footage. Dana's imminent death is no more than background entertainment and easily ignored, with the scene's spotlight firmly on the partygoers who deputise as clearly for the horror audience as the Hadley/Sitterson pairing implies the Goddard/Whedon team. What the studio considered too awful to be shown—and perhaps not only because it might eat into its profits—was the idea of a film guilt-tripping an audience who paid to watch it. As Whedon's and Goddard's grim battle to hold on to the scene shows, this is also what mattered most to them.

Like the film whose centrepiece it is, the party sequence 'is not only a critique, but a confession.'[24] As such it is also the scene that most eloquently contradicts the fear-theory of horror, for it is guilt, not fear, that triggers confessions. The scene's purpose is to identify moral issues, specifically people's indifference to the misery they themselves have caused, or, in a nutshell, their failure to feel guilty. Hadley's fleeting moment of sympathy for Dana, which introduces the scene, also exemplifies it in that his musings about her anguish fail to consider his own role in bringing it about.

Yet this is not merely an indictment-by-proxy of a movie audience who triggers horrors by paying the price of admission but does not pay for its viewing pleasures in coin of guilt. The question the party sequence implies is the one Whedon asked directly in his blog about the 'honour' killing of Du'a Khalil Aswad, acerbically entitled 'Let's Watch a Girl Get Beaten to Death': why we respond to the suffering of others with either prurient interest or bored indifference, rather than—as well we should—with compassion, moral outrage and immediate action. As Whedon points out in his blog and as Goddard and Whedon point out in their film, we do this whether the savagery is factual or fictional. Like Dana at the party, real-life victims are so often no more than grainy people on shaky screens, brought to you by news stations around the world: people running from bombs or shelling in Syria, Iraq or Libya; the dead or maimed being dug out of the rubble of a bombed hospital in Yemen; screaming demonstrators being tear-gassed, beaten or flung into unmarked vans in Washington, Portland, Oregon or Hong Kong, by armed police or military sent to do this by their own governments; refugees drowning in rickety boats in the Mediterranean sea or being caged at the Mexico–US border; Covid-victims flung into mass graves all over the world. Our response to these nightly horrors may be worthier than 'pass the pretzels, dear,' but rarely rises to the acknowledgement that we have caused all this through indifference, laziness, environmental carelessness, overconsumption, neglect of our civic duties and insistence on our rights at other people's expense, much less to a change in these behaviours.

Cabin's party scene is a study of how people comport themselves when they know they're causing the death of others but either don't care or find a 'cause' to justify it, an exploration of how humans behave when they think their misdeeds won't have any consequences for them. In this, of course, the revellers are gravely mistaken, for in the end, the film's 'classic dénouement' unleashes every horror critter imaginable on them, affording us the chance to watch (or ignore) their colourful deaths with the same indifference with which they watched (or, more usually, ignored) Dana's devastation during the party. We the horror audience are implicated both in the office workers whose party behaviour we emulate when it's their turn to be messily killed, and in the Evil Gods, who—like us—are watching on both levels and who—like us—are 'customers' who must be kept 'satisfied.' Is it any wonder that the Evil God's hand swatting at the viewer in the film's final shot is humanly formed? It is, as Canavan has remarked, 'the final mirror in a film that is filled with them; in the end, when the Old Ones rise to wreak their unfathomable havoc upon the world, there is nothing but our own hands reaching out for us.'[25]

Was it this that garnered *Cabin* some reviews that went well beyond the normal range of professional disapproval, denunciations that, like a slasher movie, went straight for the jugular? Before the film was even made, a script reviewer suggested that the project was kept '"top secret" […] because if anyone laid their eyes on this piece of crap, they'd throw it into the fires of Hell before allowing it to get made.' The article teems with insults ('piece of crap,' 'trash,' 'really stupid,' 'a joke'), expletives ('… this is where I honestly said "fuck you" to my computer') and boasts no fewer than two instances of 'give me a fucking break.'[26]

Such impressive abandonment of professionalism bespeaks not merely censure but a considerable degree of defensiveness; the linguistic behaviour is not that of a critic finding fault but that of someone warding off a personal attack. It is an extreme example of a more general tendency in reviewing and ranking behaviours identified by Murray Smith:

> Some kinds of fiction elicit univocal, or mixed but complementary, emotional responses, while others invite conflicting and ambiguous emotional responses, and this division corresponds in general to the ranking of what our society deems 'serious fiction' (or 'art') over 'mere fantasy' or 'entertainment'. And all too often this dichotomy is assumed to be isomorphic with a divide between 'Hollywood movies' and 'art films'. But this is surely a contingent relationship—one with a history which one might begin tracing in the development of the novel. Some fictions which elicit strong emotional responses are lauded for their sincerity and profundity, others— usually when they effect an imaginative recasting of the spectator's beliefs and values in a direction that they do not like—are rejected as 'manipulative'.[27]

Perhaps this explains why horror in general is so commonly considered the lowest of all cinematic artforms, and why *Cabin* in particular has been called all sorts of names (manipulative, unoriginal, trite, boring, a piece of crap): by holding up a mirror to its spectators' ugly faces, it recasts their beliefs and values in a direction that they do not like.

The Cabin in the Woods is a horror film on an ethical mission and guilt-trips its viewers with that mission in mind. It is also, in this respect, quite typical for the horror genre, which is why I would read *Cabin* as a belated prototype for its own genre. To an audience raised on the idea that you're supposed to be scared when watching a horror film, this may seem counter-intuitive. But think of all the horror films that routinely send their viewers on guilt trips by pointing directly at the guilty involvement of their *audience*. Think of all the mad scientist movies, rape-of-nature films, films about consumerism or child abuse. The most famous horror films ever made are, without exception, thematic guilt trips. *The Exorcist* (1973), *Carrie* (1976) and *The Shining* (1980) are all visceral films about child abuse, barely masking this with an ostentatious focus on religion or the supernatural. *Poltergeist* (1982), in which a child is pulled into a television by evil spirits, visualises America's deterioration into a society of zombies hypnotised by TV. *Child's Play* (1988), with its stark contrasts of poverty and commercially bought happiness, and George Romero's *Dawn of the Dead* (1978), with its hordes of blank-eyed shopping mall zombies, are direct attacks on American consumerism. In *Children of the Corn* (1984), the children in a small farming community murder all adults in the town for 'defiling the corn' (read: destroying the planet) through pesticides and other forms of irresponsible farming. Ibañez Serrador's 1976 film *¿Quién puede matar a un niño?* (*Who Can Kill a Child?*) explicitly casts the murder of all adults at the hands of the children on a small Spanish island as revenge for the wholesale and worldwide slaughter of children in wars, famines and acts of ethnic cleansing. Horror films *always* Know What We Did Last Summer. Whether or not they blare this at us in their titles, most films make no bones about the fact that fear, while certainly present, is no more than incidental, a side dish. The main item on horror's menu is *guilt*.

Perhaps this also explains the prevalence of sequels, which are more ubiquitous in horror than in any other genre. Horror sequels are not about confronting viewers with the new and unknown but about sending viewers *back* to something they already know—back into the same dank cellar, the same haunted house, the same nightmare.[28]

An old fear becomes less troubling as it becomes more familiar. Not so an old guilt, which becomes not less, but more tormenting with increased familiarity. Sequels that typically tell the same story all over again are a signal that guilt can only be repressed for so long, that like Michael Myers, the Blob or the Thing, it keeps coming back, and that unlike fear, it cannot be overcome.

If horror films are, as I've argued elsewhere as well,[29] more about guilt than fear, the question arises: where is the pleasure in watching horror? We all understand the pleasures of fear, particularly vicarious fear experienced from a position of safety. But is there any fun to be had with guilt? Evidence from other fields has suggested an affirmative answer. Recent marketing research, for example, has firmly established that guilty pleasures are the best. Goldsmith, Cho and Dhar conducted six interrelated studies to prove that there is a fundamental cognitive association between guilt and pleasure. Their studies show not only that people primed with guilt experience greater pleasure than others, but also that the effect of heightening the enjoyment of pleasures is unique to guilt. Other negative emotions, in other words, do not result in the same enjoyment; *only* guilt works in this way. What is more, two of their studies show that the pleasurable guilt trip is not limited to consumption of guilt-inducing foods, such as candy, but applies to other contexts as well. One of their examples for what they call 'hedonic consumption,' a form of consumption in which guilt enhances pleasure, is watching videos.

If marketing research gives us an idea of how we enjoy guilt, philosophy can perhaps get us a bit closer to the 'why.' This is the point where we need to ask whether the viewer's allegiance to a film character is wholly determined by ethical stances. The question of ethics and identification is a particularly hairy one in horror films. Evil is the real deal; the monster is horror's real hero. Good, as far as the genre is concerned, can take a hike in the woods, preferably on a dark and stormy night. So often, the struggle against Evil is against something undefined and indefinable (the Thing, the Blob, the Slime). Not having a concrete enemy deprives the struggler of nobility, of the ability to win, and of the *meaning* of victory: where is the dignity in escaping, temporarily, from encroaching slime? Good takes one of two guises: horror's many victims—for whom viewers can hardly even muster sympathy—or, more rarely, an antagonist, a 'zero hero'[30] who, like the victims, is hapless, dimwitted, laughably inadequate to the task, and always at least ten steps behind Evil.

Nevertheless, there is reason to suspect that the horror film's (and viewers') greater interest in Evil is more than a default position arrived at by the exquisite boredom caused by Good: it is a matter of identification. Once we understand that horror is more about guilt than fear, it becomes possible to read viewer identification with Evil as a way to overcome fear. Identifying with Evil may result in guilt, but at least it propels the viewer from the place of Fear, the victim's position—always held by Good, in horror—and into a position of power. Some philosophers have, in fact, built a fundamental definition of Evil on this. C. Fred Alford, for example, has shown that if the desire to combat fear is a natural impulse, then identification with Evil is not an aberration but simply a human trait, a 'psychopathic moment' that everyone experiences:

> The psychopathic moment is a virtually universal moment in all lives. When we are faced with intolerable, uncontainable dread, the natural tendency is to identify with the persecutor, becoming the agent of doom, as the only way of controlling it. Evil is the attempt to inflict one's doom on others, becoming doom, rather than living subject to it. In this sense evil is bad faith, the lie that one could escape one's fate by inflicting it on others.[31]

Transferring Alford's insights from the lofty heights of philosophy to the damp dungeons of horror shows us *why* horror films concern themselves more with guilt than with fear. Horror films are fictionalised psychopathic moments in which viewers are faced with the alternative between fear and guilt and the option to choose guilt as the safer route. To identify with the persecutor is the only way to avoid being terrified. We pay for our rejection of fear (the victim's position) in coin of guilt (by assuming the perp's position), and guilt, Alford declares, will not sway us: 'most of us feel guilty, at least sometimes. Neither guilt nor empathy will change this tendency to inflict terror on others, however.'[32] Terror as defined by Alford is not fear (of Evil) but guilt—the terror of recognising *ourselves* as evil. 'We do not feel terror and *then* identify with the aggressor, or at least that is not the whole story. The terror stems *from* the identification with the aggressor, his aggression suddenly our own, directed against those we care about and depend on, including ourselves and our values.'[33] And that, I think, is the second central aspect of horror: not only does it showcase the 'psychopathic moment' when the viewer may choose guilt over fear, it also digs its fingers into the gaping wound created by the viewer's simultaneous alignment with Evil (in *Cabin*'s case, the Downstairs crew or the Evil Gods) and presumed allegiance to Good (*Cabin*'s teens).

If Goldsmith, Cho and Dhar's conclusion that 'Guilt Begets Pleasure' is right, we are looking at the perfect vicious circle. Not only does watching schlock horror, if we find that sort of thing pleasurable, cause guilt, the reverse also applies: guilt enhances the hedonistic pleasure of watching horror. If the main point of horror is not fear but guilt, it is simply because guilt works. It works for the horror film because fear is fleeting but guilt lasts. It works for the viewer because, paradoxically, guilt offers greater pleasures than fear. And if Alford's conclusion that we will always fall victim to the psychopathic moment is right, we can go a step further and say: horror films guilt-trip viewers not only by enticing them to identify with the guilty party, but also by pointing out that this is the viewer's default position. It is not merely a trick of the I-camera (the horror genre's favourite ploy: visual identification of killer and audience through the killer's point-of-view), but identification in the sense of *allegiance*. It is not due to manipulation by the movie, or at least not entirely, but a decision made by the viewer who chooses guilt over fear. And it is *pleasurable*. It is precisely the kind of nasty secret that we shouldn't put past the genre. In the sober world of market research and in the airy palaces of philosophy, probing the pleasures of guilt may be new, unexpected, even controversial. But in the darker places where guilt links with the imagination—the Catholic confessional, the horror cinema—the pleasures of guilt may well have been familiar to wallowers all along.

This is how horror is out to get you: by proclaiming you guilty and by pointing out that you like it that way. Pleading mitigating circumstances or diminished culpability—after all, you didn't do it, you only watched—won't get you off the hook. And if you now, as would be entirely understandable, ask the fallback question of the desperate: *Why Me?*, horror would answer: Nothing personal. You are just the one who showed up, just like some horny teens always show up at the cabin in the woods. The real question is: why *did* you show up? Why do you crave horror stories? Why do you *need* horror stories? *Why do you look?* The question is still unanswerable, but it is not senseless to ask it, just as it is not senseless to look, because horror is on purpose. Guilt is on purpose. Evil is on purpose. Pain is on purpose, as the universe informs Rick, another character trapped in cataclysmic events:

> Rick will ask both himself and the cosmos, *Why is it that the only way we ever seem to take steps forward in life is through pain? Why is exposure to pain supposed to make us better people?* And the universe, like a cosmic high school principal speaking over a celestial PA system, will tell him, 'Well, Richard, good things don't change people, and what is the point of doing anything if you're not going to change?'[34]

Notes

1. Stephen King, 'Why We Crave Horror Movies.'
2. Joss Whedon's question is quoted in Kowalski, *Joss Whedon as Philosopher* 192.
3. I include myself in this long line of baffled writers; my *Little Horrors*, from which some of the arguments and conclusions in this chapter are taken, is one long engagement with the why-question (see particularly the book's Introduction and Conclusion).
4. Lemire 4.
5. Canavan, 'Nightmares' para. 34.
6. Alan Jones ix.
7. This is the title of the seminal anthology edited by Steffen Hantke.
8. Muir 1.
9. Davis and Natale 38; see also McCown: 'A horror film's primary job is to deliver scares' (quoted in McLevy and James); A. O. Scott: 'We go to scary movies because we enjoy being manipulated into being scared by phenomena we know better than to believe in'; Sterba: 'Horror movies aim to scare' (144) and countless others.
10. Lovecraft, *Supernatural Horror* 12.
11. Repetition and familiarity are expressed not only in the horror narrative but also in its franchising. No cinematic genre is as prone to sequelitis as horror. There are now 12 *Friday the 13th*s, 13 *Halloween*s, 14 *Puppet Master*s, 9 *Nightmares on Elm Street*, 11 *Hellraiser*s, and 9 *Saw*s, to name only the most famous. As anyone who has ever seen one of these can attest, sequels of horror films are not actually different films but the same film all over again, and appropriately so, since all horror films are fundamentally predictable. The predictability is not perceived as boring; it is, in fact, expected and relied upon. Part of the pleasure of

watching a horror film is that you know exactly what is coming, which, in other film genres, like the thriller or detective genres, spells the very opposite of suspense.

12. See, among many others: Bradshaw ('however smart and sophisticated this film is, it may disappoint those who, in their hearts, would still like to be genuinely scared'); Buckwalter ('Neither is the movie particularly scary'); Ebert ('"The Cabin in the Woods" does have some genuine scares, but they're not really the point'); Edelstein ('Is it scary? Not especially'); Goldman ('The Cabin in the Woods is rarely scary,' from 'Lurking in the Darkness'); Hartlaub ('Scares are sacrificed for humor and awesomeness'); McCown ('I agree that it's not the scariest film ever,' quoted in McLevy and James); Schwarzbaum ('In these Woods, the honest terror of real horror is never a threat'); Sharkey ('The laughs come easily, the screams not so much'); and Stevens ('practically never scary').

13. See Curran.

14. Aristotle, Poetics, chs 1, 4, 6–8.

15. As noted in Blouin, 'Growing Global Darkness' 95; Canavan, 'Nightmares' para. 18; Debruge; Ebert; Giannini, 'Charybdis' para. 18; Hosogi para. 4; Kooyman 101 and 108; Mayo 241; Parrish para. 24; Renner 118–19; Richardson 4, 33–4, 43, 50; A. O. Scott; Sessarego; Starr para. 22; Woofter and Stokes paras 4, 9; Woofter 277–8.

16. Whedon, The Cabin in the Woods: The Official Visual Companion 149.

17. Whedon, cited in Giannini, 'Nightmares' para. 15.

18. Bridget McGovern comes close to questioning the fear-theory in her review of Cabin, but in the end finds nothing to replace it with: 'I'd argue that the genius of The Cabin in the Woods lies precisely in the fact that it leads its audience to question what the genre has become, and what we're getting out of it. If horror movies are a safe way of exploring fears both primal and cultural, what do we really need to be afraid of, *now*, in 2012? It's not the escaped maniac with a hook haunting lovers' lanes, and it's not Leatherface (or Deadites, or an off-brand Pinhead, or even a rampaging killer unicorn)… turns out, the new face of ultimate evil is two pasty, middle-aged guys in a golf cart. Or at least, it's what they represent' (unpag.).

19. Claimed by Kowalski in *Joss Whedon as Philosopher* 197.

20. My translation of Moldenhauer, 'Pigs' 30: 'CABIN will das wissende Kichern des Genrekenners wieder durch eine neue Ernsthaftigkeit (wie auch, nicht zuletzt, durch bessere Witze) ersetzt wissen.'

21. Goddard's comment is taken from an interview with the *A.V. Club* and quoted in Giannini, 'Charybdis' para. 27.

22. Related by Pascale 328.

23. See particularly Karen Renner on this scene (118–19).

24. Richardson 8.
25. Canavan, 'Nightmares' para. 40.
26. *The Cabin in the Woods* script review in *Scriptshadow*.
27. Smith 229.
28. This may also be why horror films are so often compared with nightmares, which are also often manifestations of guilt or bad conscience.
29. In my *Little Horrors* (2016).
30. I owe Stephen King for the lovely term, coined in *Danse Macabre* (441).
31. Alford 58.
32. Alford 59.
33. Alford 59.
34. Douglas Coupland, *Player One* 85 (emphasis original).

Bibliography / Filmography

Alford, C. Fred. *What Evil Means to Us*. Ithaca: Cornell UP, 1997.

Aristotle. *Aristotle's Poetics*. Ed. Stephen Halliwell. Chicago: U of Chicago P, 1998.

Baer, John, James C. Kaufman and Roy F. Baumeister. *Are We Free? Psychology and Free Will*. Oxford, New York: Oxford UP, 2008.

Barker, Clive (dir.). *Hellraiser*. Feature Film. Cinemarque Entertainment BV (1987).

Barton, Charles T. (dir.). *Abbott and Costello Meet Frankenstein*. Feature Film. Universal International Pictures (1948).

Barton, Steve. 'Motion Picture Purgatory: The Cabin in the Woods.' *Dread Central* (24 May 2012). https://www.dreadcentral.com/news/34069/motion-picture-purgatory-the-cabin-in-the-woods/

Bergson, Henri. *Time and Free Will*. Trans. F. L. Pogson. London: George Allen & Unwin, 1959.

Blouin, Michael J. 'American Horror, Global Commons, and *The Cabin in the Woods*.' *Magical Thinking, Fantastical Film, and the Illusions of Neoliberalism*. New York: Macmillan, 2016. 139–68.

Blouin, Michael J. 'Research Cluster—"A Growing Global Darkness": Dialectics of Culture in Goddard's *The Cabin in the Woods*.' *Horror Studies* 6/1 (2015): 83–99.

Blumenau, Ralph. 'Free Will & Predestination.' *Philosophy Now* 20 (Spring 1998): 20–2.

Bradshaw, Peter. '*The Cabin in the Woods*: This Clever Meta-Horror Asks What Human Need Is Fed by Seeing Hot Youths Get Slaughtered, But It Forgets to Be Properly Scary.' *The Guardian* (12 April 2012). https://www.theguardian.com/film/2012/apr/12/the-cabin-in-the-woods-review

Brophy, Philip. 'Horrality: The Textuality of Contemporary Horror Films.' *Screen* 27/1 (1986): 2–13.

Buckwalter, Ian. '*Cabin in the Woods*: A Dead-Serious Genre Exorcism.' *NPR* (12 April 2012). https://www.npr.org/2012/04/12/150299147/cabin-in-the-woods-a-dead-serious-genre-exorcism?t=1585235773950

Burr, Ty. '*Cabin* Takes a Whack at Clever Horror.' *Boston Globe* (13 April 2012).

'The Cabin in the Woods (2011): External Reviews.' https://www.imdb.com/title/tt1259521/externalreviews

'The Cabin in the Woods (2011): The Final Girl Podcast' (28 August 2020). https://music.amazon.co.uk/podcasts/3e59755b-1866-4cbd-8e64-06ad4fe23587/episodes/84592c06-c748-4862-a405-0b249df204da/the-final-girl-podcast-the-cabin-in-the-woods-2011

'*The Cabin in the Woods* (Script)—Review.' *TV Calling*. https://www.tv-calling.com/the-cabin-in-the-woods-script-review/

The Cabin in the Woods. *Scriptshadow: Reviewing the Latest Scripts in Hollywood* (2 March 2009). http://scriptshadow.net/the-cabin-in-the-woods/

The Cabin in the Woods. Wikipedia site. https://en.wikipedia.org/wiki/The_Cabin_in_the_Woods

Cameron, James (dir.). *Aliens*. Feature Film. Twentieth Century Fox (1986).

Canavan, Gerry. '"Something Nightmares Are From": Metacommentary in Joss Whedon's *The Cabin in the Woods*.' *Slayage: The Journal of Whedon Studies* 36/37 (Fall 2013/Winter 2014). https://www.whedonstudies.tv/uploads/2/6/2/8/26288593/canavan_slayage_10.2-11.1.pdf

Canavan, Gerry. 'You Think You Know the Story: Novelty, Repetition and Lovecraft in Whedon and Goddard's *The Cabin in the Woods*.' *The Politics of Adaptation: Media Convergion and Ideology*. Ed. Dan Hassler-Forest and Pascal Nicklas. New York: Macmillan, 2015. 201–13.

Carpenter, John (dir.). *Big Trouble in Little China*. Feature Film. Twentieth Century Fox (1986).

Carpenter, John (dir.). *Halloween*. Feature Film. Compass International Pictures (1978).

Carpenter, John (dir.). *The Thing*. Feature Film. Universal Pictures (1982).

Carroll, Noël. 'Horror and Humor.' *The Journal of Aesthetics and Art Criticism* 57/2 (1999): 145–60.

Caruso, Gregg D. *Free Will and Consciousness: A Determinist Account of the Illusion of Free Will*. Lanham, MD: Lexington Books, 2012.

Caterall, Ali. 'Iron Sky / The Cabin in the Woods.' *The Word* (May 2012): 88.

Charity, Tom. 'Review: *Cabin in the Woods* Is Sheer Horror Heaven.' *CNN* (13 April 2012).

Cherry, Brigid. *Horror*. London: Routledge, 2009.

Clayton, Wickham, ed. *Style and Form in the Hollywood Slasher Film*. Houndmills, Basingstoke: Palgrave Macmillan, 2015.

Clevver Movies. 'Joss Whedon *The Cabin in the Wood* [sic] Interview. *YouTube*. https://www.youtube.com/watch?v=hBt5q1snJs4

Clover, Carol J. *Men, Women, and Chain Saws: Gender in the Modern Horror Film*. Princeton: Princeton UP, 1992.

Collis, Clark. '*The Cabin in the Woods*: How Joss Whedon and Drew Goddard's "Insane Frolic" Became the Year's Most Buzzed-About Fright Flick.' *Entertainment Weekly* 12 (April 2012).

Conaton, Chris. 'Joss Whedon 101: *The Cabin in the Woods*.' *Joss Whedon: The Complete Companion. The TV Series, the Movies, the Comic Books and More*. London: Titan, 2012. 440–2.

Cooper, L. Andrew. '*The Cabin in the Woods* and the End of American Exceptionalism.' *Slayage: The Journal of Whedon Studies* 36/37 (Fall 2013/Winter 2014). https://www.whedonstudies.tv/uploads/2/6/2/8/26288593/cooper_slayage_10.2-11.1.pdf https://www.researchgate.net/publication/309653648_The_Cabin_in_the_Woods_and_the_End_of_American_Exceptionalism

Coupland, Douglas. *Player One: What Is to Become of Us. A Novel in Five Hours*. London: Heinemann, 2010.

Craven, Wes (dir.). *The Hills Have Eyes*. Feature Film. Blood Relations Company (1977).

Craven, Wes (dir.). *Scream*. Feature Film. Dimension Films (1996).

Cunningham, Sean S. (dir.). *Friday the 13th*. Feature Film. Paramount Pictures (1980).

Curran, Angela. 'Brecht's Criticisms of Aristotle's Aesthetics of Tragedy.' *The Journal of Aesthetics and Art Criticism* 59/2 (Spring 2001): 167–84.

Davis, Blair, and Kial Natale. '"The Pound of Flesh Which I Demand": American Horror Cinema, Gore, and the Box Office, 1998–2007.' *American Horror Film: The Genre at the Turn of the Millennium*. Ed. Steffen Hantke. Jackson: UP of Mississippi, 2010. 35–57.

Day, Deanna. 'Toward a Zombie Epistemology: What It Means to Live and Die in *The Cabin in the Woods*.' *Ada: A Journal of Gender, New Media, and Technology* 3 (November 2013).

Debruge, Peter. '*The Cabin in the Woods:* Not Since *Scream* Has a Horror Movie Subverted the Expectations that Accompany the Genre to Such Wicked Effect.' *Variety* (9 March 2012). https://variety.com/2012/film/markets-festivals/the-cabin-in-the-woods-1117947213/

Demme, Jonathan (dir.). *The Silence of the Lambs*. Feature Film. Orion Pictures (1991).

DePalma, Brian (dir.). *Carrie*. Feature Film. Red Bank Films (1976).

Dickson, Evan. 'Brian White Talks Working with Joss Whedon and Drew Goddard on *The Cabin in the Woods*!' *Bloody Disgusting* (9 March 2012). https://bloody-disgusting.com/interviews/28670/interview-brian-white-talks-working-with-joss-whedon-and-drew-goddard-on-the-cabin-in-the-woods/

Dray, Colin. 'Burning Down the House: *The Cabin in the Woods* and Genre Immolation.' *Joss Whedon: The Complete Companion. The TV Series, the Movies, the Comic Books and More*. London: Titan, 2012. 444–8.

Ebert, Roger. 'Another Ominous Gas Station Owner: Review of *The Cabin in the Woods*.' *Chicago Sun-Times* (11 April 2012). https://www.rogerebert.com/reviews/the-cabin-in-the-woods-2012

Edelman, Lee. *No Future: Queer Theory and the Death Drive*. Durham, NC: Duke UP, 2004.

Edelstein, David. 'Review of *The Cabin in the Woods*.' *New York* (16 April 2012). https://nymag.com/movies/reviews/monsieur-lazhar-cabin-in-the-woods-2012-4/

Everett, Bryan. 'American Exceptionalism in the Film Industry of the Middle Twentieth Century.' MA Thesis (University of North Georgia, 2017). https://www.semanticscholar.org/paper/American-Exceptionalism-in-the-Film-Industry-of-the-Everett/abb807bfb5e9e8d117aedd5eaedb81ce4ce53619

Faraci, Devin. 'The Devil's Advocate: Why Are Negative Reviews Spoiling THE CABIN IN THE WOODS?' *Badass Digest* (10 Apr 2012). https://birthmoviesdeath.com/reviews

Feldman, Gilad, Roy F. Baumeister and Kin Fai Ellick Wong. 'Free Will Is About Choosing: The Link Between Choice and the Belief in Free Will.' *Journal of Experimental Social Psychology* 55 (November 2014): 239–45.

'Final Girl.' Wikipedia site. https://en.wikipedia.org/wiki/Final_girl

Fincher, David (dir.). *Alien3*. Feature Film. Twentieth Century Fox (1992).

Fischer, Russ. '*The Cabin in the Woods*: Exclusive Interview with Director Drew Goddard, and Behind the Scenes Blu-Ray clip.' *Slash Film* (18 September 2012). https://www.slashfilm.com/the-cabin-in-the-woods-exclusive-interview-with-director-drew-goddard-and-behind-the-scenes-blu-ray-clip/

Freud, Sigmund. *The Uncanny*. Trans. David McLintock. New York: Penguin Books, 2003.

Friedkin, William (dir.). *The Exorcist*. Feature Film. Warner Bros. (1973).

Friedländer, Saul, ed. *Visions of Apocalypse: End or Rebirth?* New York: Holmes & Meier, 1985.

Fuchs, Cynthia. 'The Cabin in the Woods': You've Been Here Before.' *PopMatters* (12 April 2012). https://www.popmatters.com/157199-the-cabin-in-the-woods-youve-been-here-before-2495863341.html

Genette, Gérard. *Fiction & Diction*. Trans. Catherine Porter. Ithaca: Cornell UP, 1993.

Giannini, Erin. '"Charybdis Tested Well with Teens": *The Cabin in the Woods* as Metafictional Critique of Corporate Media Producers and Audiences.' *Slayage: The Journal of Whedon Studies* 36/37 (Fall 2013/Winter 2014). http://www.whedonstudies.tv/uploads/2/6/2/8/26288593/giannini_slayage_10.2-11.1.pdf

Giannini, Erin. 'In the Belly of the Beast: *Dollhouse*, *The Cabin in the Woods* and *Dr. Horrible's Sing-Along Blog*.' *Joss Whedon Versus the Corporation: Big Business Critiqued in the Films and Television Programs*. Jefferson, NC: McFarland, 2017. 80–94.

Giannini, Erin. 'Something Nightmares Are From: Corporate Culture and Externalized Consequences.' *After the Avengers: From Joss Whedon's Hottest, Newest Franchises to the Future of the Whedonverse*. Ed. Valerie Estelle Frankel. *PopMatters* (2015; unpaginated electronic book).

Gillespie, Jim (dir.). *I Know What You Did Last Summer*. Feature Film. Mandalay Entertainment (1997).

Gingold, Michael. 'Review: THE CABIN IN THE WOODS. An Archive Review from The Gingold Files.' *Fangoria* (9 March 2019). https://www.fangoria.com/original/review-the-cabin-in-the-woods/

Goddard, Drew (dir.). *The Cabin in the Woods*. Feature Film. Lionsgate Films (2012).

Goldman, Eric. '*The Cabin in the Woods*: What's Truly Lurking in the Darkness.' *IGN* (12 April 2012, updated 23 October 2020). https://www.ign.com/articles/2012/04/12/the-cabin-in-the-woods-review

Goldman, Eric. "Cabin in the Woods Maze Announced for Halloween Horror Nights at Universal Studios Florida." *IGN* (1 July 2013). https://uk.ign.com/articles/2013/07/01/cabin-in-the-woods-maze-announced-for-halloween-horror-nights-at-universal-studios-florida

Goldsmith, Kelly, Eunice Kim Cho and Ravi Dhar. 'When Guilt Begets Pleasure: The Positive Effect of a Negative Emotion.' *Journal of Marketing Research* XLIX (December 2012): 872–81.

Graves, Stephanie. 'Inscription and Subversion: *The Cabin in the Woods* and the Postmodern Horror Tradition.' *Joss Whedon vs. the Horror Tradition: The Production of Genre in Buffy and Beyond*. Ed. Kristopher Karl Woofter and Lorna Jowett. London: I. B. Tauris, 2019. Unpag.

Grissemann, Stefan, and Michael Omasta. 'Herr Haneke, wo bleibt das Positive? Ein Gespräch mit dem Regisseur.' *Der siebente Kontinent: Michael Haneke und seine Filme*. Ed. Alexander Horwath. Vienna, Zurich: Europaverlag, 1991. 193–214.

G-Wing. Comment on the YouTube version of Haneke's opening sequence (US version). https://www.youtube.com/watch?v=zfwJiG2F698

Hall, Stuart. 'Encoding / Decoding.' *Culture, Media, Language*. Ed. Stuart Hall, Dorothy Hobson, Andrew Lowe and Paul Willis. London: Hutchinson, 1980. 128–39.

Hallam, Scott. 'Cabin in the Woods, The (Blu-ray/DVD).' Review. *Dread Central* (16 September 2012). https://www.dreadcentral.com/reviews/37499/cabin-in-the-woods-the-blu-ray-dvd/

Hammond, Collin. 'We Are Not Who We Are: Metahorror's Examination of Genre and Audience.' *The Ashen Egg: A Journal of Undergraduate English Scholarship* 3 (2015): 25–35.

Haneke, Michael (dir.). *Funny Games*. Feature Film. ORF (Austria 1997); Celluloid Dreams (USA 2007).

Hantke, Steffen, ed. *Horror Film: Creating and Marketing Fear*. Jackson: UP of Mississippi, 2004.

Hartlaub, Peter. 'Review of *The Cabin in the Woods*.' *San Francisco Chronicle* (13 April 2012, updated 6 August 2013). https://www.sfgate.com/movies/article/Cabin-in-the-Woods-review-3477920.php

Hill, George Roy (dir.). *Butch Cassidy and the Sundance Kid*. Feature Film. Campanile Productions (1969).

Holland, Jesse, and Andy Mitton (dirs). *YellowBrickRoad*. Feature Film. Points North Films (2010).

Holland, Tom (dir.). *Child's Play*. Feature Film. United Artists (1988).

Hooper, Tobe (dir.). *Poltergeist*. Feature Film. MGM (1982).

Hooper, Tobe (dir.). *The Texas Chain Saw Massacre*. Feature Film. Vortex (1974).

Hornaday, Ann. 'Review of *The Cabin in the Woods*.' *The Washington Post* (12 April 2012).

'Horror Films Referenced in *The Cabin in the Woods*.' *IMDb* (23 October 2016). https://www.imdb.com/list/ls066732149/

'Horror Movie Budgets Are Getting Smaller.' *Where's the Jump?* (2020). https://wheresthejump.com/horror-movie-budgets-are-getting-smaller/

Hosogi, Michelle. 'Tequila Is My Lady: Is *The Cabin in the Woods* Nihilistically Half Full?' *Watcher Junior* 11 (Spring 2015). http://www.whedonstudies.tv/uploads/2/6/2/8/26288593/hosogi_watcherjunior_8.1.pdf

Huxley, Aldous. *Brave New World*. New York: RosettaBooks, 2000.

'I Don't Know Much Latin, But I'm Pretty Sure the Latin in *The Cabin in the Woods* Is Wrong.' *reddit* (2015). https://www.reddit.com/r/latin/comments/2e8rhf/i_dont_know_much_latin_but_im_pretty_sure_the/

'I Learned It By Watching You!' PSA anti-drug ad. *YouTube*. https://www.youtube.com/watch?v=KUXb7do9C-w

It. TV Mini-Series. ITV Studios (1990).

Jackson, Kimberly. 'Meta-horror and Simulation in the *Scream* Series and *The Cabin in the Woods*.' *Technology, Monstrosity, and Reproduction in Twenty-First Century Horror*. New York: Macmillan, 2013. 11–30.

Jeunet, Jean-Pierre (dir.). *Alien: Resurrection*. Feature Film. Twentieth Century Fox (1997).

Jones, Alan. *The Rough Guide to Horror Movies*. London: Penguin, 2005.

Jones, J. R. 'Review of *The Cabin in the Woods*.' *Chicago Reader* (12 April 2012). https://www.chicagoreader.com/chicago/the-cabin-in-the-woods/Film?oid=6031396

Kane, Robert. *A Contemporary Introduction to Free Will*. Oxford, New York: Oxford UP, 2005.

Kane, Robert. *The Significance of Free Will*. Oxford, New York: Oxford UP, 1998.

Kiersch, Fritz (dir.). *Children of the Corn*. Feature Film. New World Pictures (1984).

King, Derrick. 'The (Bio)political Economy of Bodies, Culture as Commodification, and the Badiouian Event: Reading Political Allegories in *The Cabin in the Woods*.' *Slayage: The Journal of Whedon Studies* 38/39 (Summer 2014). http://www.whedonstudies.tv/uploads/2/6/2/8/26288593/king_slayage_11.2-12.1.pdf

King, Stephen. *Danse Macabre*. London: Warner Books, 1991.

King, Stephen. 'Why We Crave Horror Movies.' http://drmarkwomack.com/pdfs/why_we_crave_horror_movies.pdf

Kooyman, Ben. '"Gotta Keep the Customer Satisfied": Puppeteers as Director-surrogates in *The Cabin in the Woods*.' *Horror Studies* 6/1 (2015): 101–19.

Kord, T. S. 'Gangs and Guilt: Towards a New Theory of Horror Film.' *Cultural Dynamics* 28/1 (March 2016): 69–83.

Kord, T. S. *Little Horrors: How Cinema's Evil Children Play on Our Guilt*. Jefferson, NC: McFarland, 2016.

Kowalski, Dean A. *Joss Whedon as Philosopher*. Lanham: Lexington, 2017.

Kowalski, Dean A., and S. Evan Kreider. 'Introduction.' *The Philosophy of Joss Whedon*. Ed. Dean A. Kowalski and S. Evan Kreider. Lexington: UP of Kentucky, 2011. 1–5.

Kowalski, Dean A., and S. Evan Kreider (eds.). *The Philosophy of Joss Whedon*. Lexington: UP of Kentucky, 2011.

Krenn, Günter. 'Michael und die Alpha-Kunst: Praktische Gedanken der Cutterin Monika Willi und des Kameramannes Christian Berger zu Michael Hanekes Modus Operandi.' *Film-Konzepte 21: Michael Haneke* (February 2011): 76–91.

Kubrick, Stanley (dir.). *Dr. Strangelove or: How I Learned to Stop Worrying and Love the Bomb*. Feature Film. Columbia Pictures (1964).

Kubrick, Stanley (dir.). *The Shining*. Feature Film. Warner Bros (1980).

Lamberson, Greg (dir.). *Slime City* (alternate: *The Slime*). Feature Film. Bare Bones Productions (1988).

Lavery, David. '*The Cabin in the Woods*.' *Joss Whedon, A Creative Portrait: From* Buffy the Vampire Slayer *to Marvel's* The Avengers. New York: I. B. Tauris, 2014. 149–53.

Lebbon, Tim. *The Cabin in the Woods: The Official Movie Novelization*. London: Titan, 2012.

Leffel, Jim, and Dennis McCallum. 'The Postmodern Challenge, Facing the Spirit of the Age.' *Christian Research Institute* (2001). https://www.equip.org/articles/the-postmodern-challenge/

Lemire, Christy. 'The Cabin in the Woods.' *Philadelphia Tribune* (20 April 2012): 3–4.

LeRoy, Mervyn (dir.). *The Bad Seed*. Feature Film. Warner Bros (1956).

Levy, Shawn. '*The Cabin in the Woods*: A Slasher Movie with (Puppet) Strings Attached.' *Oregonian* (12 April 2012). https://www.oregonlive.com/madaboutmovies/2012/04/the_cabin_in_the_woods_review.html

Lipsett, Joe. '"One for the horror fans" vs. "An insult to the horror genre": Negotiating Reading Strategies in IMDb Reviews of *The Cabin in the Woods*.' *Slayage: The Journal of Whedon Studies* 36/37 (Fall 2013/Winter 2014). https://www.whedonstudies.tv/uploads/2/6/2/8/26288593/lipsett_slayage_10.2-11.1.pdf

Lockett, Christopher. '"We Are Not Who We Are": Lovecraftian Conspiracy and Magical Humanism in *The Cabin in the Woods*.' *Horror Studies* 6/1 (2015): 121–39.

Lovecraft, H. P. (Howard Phillips). 'The Call of Cthulhu.' Orig. 1928. http://www.hplovecraft.com/writings/texts/fiction/cc.aspx

Lovecraft, H. P. *Supernatural Horror in Literature*. New York: Dover, 1973.

Lovecraft, H. P. *Tales*. 2nd ed. New York: Library of America, 2005.

Manjikian, Mary. *Apocalypse and Post-Politics: The Romance of the End*. Lanham, MD: Lexington, 2012.

Mayo, Andrea E. 'Sacrificing Youth for a Fabricated Humanity: Governance, Youth, and Onto-Theology in *The Cabin in the Woods*.' *International Journal of Organization Theory and Behavior* 17/2 (2014): 236–63.

McCann, Ben, and David Sorfa. 'Introduction.' *The Cinema of Michael Haneke*. Ed. Ben McCann and David Sorfa. New York: Wallflower P, 2011. 1–9.

McCloud, Scott. *Understanding Comics: The Invisible Art*. New York: Harper Perennial, 1994.

McDonald, Rick. 'Sacred Violence and *The Cabin in the Woods*.' *Slayage: The Journal of Whedon Studies* 36/37 (Fall 2013/Winter 2014). https://www.whedonstudies.tv/uploads/2/6/2/8/26288593/mcdonald_slayage_10.2-11.1.pdf

McGovern, Bridget. 'Joss Whedon, John Hughes, and Torture Porn: What *The Cabin in the Woods* Says About the Current State of Pop Culture.' *Tor.com* (23 April 2012). https://www.tor.com/2012/04/23/joss-whedon-john-hughes-and-torture-porn-what-the-cabin-in-the-woods-says-about-the-current-state-of-pop-culture/

McLevy, Alex, and Becca James. 'Is *The Cabin in the Woods* a Horror Movie?' *AV Club* (29 October 2015). https://film.avclub.com/is-the-cabin-in-the-woods-a-horror-movie-1798285941

McNaughtan, Don. *The Whedonverse Catalog: A Complete Guide to Works in All Media*. Jefferson, NC: McFarland, 2018.

Metz, Jerry D. 'What's Your Fetish?: The Tortured Economics of Horror Simulacra in *The Cabin in the Woods*.' *Slayage: The Journal of Whedon Studies* 36/37 (Fall 2013/Winter 2014). https://www.whedonstudies.tv/uploads/2/6/2/8/26288593/metzjr_slayage_10.2-11.1.pdf

Meyer, Nicholas (dir.). *Star Trek II: The Wrath of Khan*. Feature Film. Paramount Pictures (1982).

Moldenhauer, Benjamin. 'Somatische Empathie und Genrekritik im Horrorfilm: *The Cabin in the Woods* (2012) und *Peeping Tom* (1960).' *Sinnlichkeit und Sinn im Kino: Zur Interdependenz von Körperlichkeit und Textualität in der Filmrezeption*. Ed. Heinz-Peter Preusser. Marburg: Schüren, 2015. 181–202.

Moldenhauer, Benjamin. '"We Get What Pigs Deserve": Selbstreflexivität und Genrekritik in *The Cabin in the Woods*.' *Zeitschrift für Fantastikforschung* 4/2 (2014): 16–32.

Morgenstern, Joe. 'A "Cabin" Stocked With Scares, Style and Smarts.' *Wall Street Journal* (12 April 2012). https://www.wsj.com/articles/SB10001424052702304446045773396120997460 68

Muccino, Gabriele (dir.). *The Pursuit of Happyness*. Feature Film. Columbia Pictures (2006).

Muir, Kenneth. *Horror Films of the 1980s*. Jefferson, NC: McFarland, 2007.

Mulvey, Laura. 'Visual Pleasure in Narrative Cinema.' *Screen* 16/3 (Autumn 1975): 6–18. http://www.asu.edu/courses/fms504/total-readings/mulvey-visualpleasure.pdf

Murphy, Bernice M. *The Rural Gothic in American Popular Culture: Backwoods Horror and Terror in the Wilderness*. New York: Palgrave Macmillan, 2013.

Myrick, Daniel, and Eduardo Sánchez (dirs.). *The Blair Witch Project*. Feature Film. Haxan Films (1999).

Nelson, Andrew Patrick. '*Trick 'r Treat*, *The Cabin in the Woods*, and the Defense of Horror's Subcultural Capital: A Genre in Crisis?' *Slayage: The Journal of Whedon Studies* 36/37 (Fall 2013/Winter 2014). https://www.whedonstudies.tv/uploads/2/6/2/8/26288593/nelson_slayage_10.2-11.1.pdf

Neumaier, Joe. '*The Cabin in the Woods* with Chris Hemsworth Gives Fun Twists to Familiar Horror.' *New York Daily News* (12 April 2012).

Newman, Kim. 'Film Review: *The Cabin in the Woods*.' *Sight & Sound* (20 December 2011). http://old.bfi.org.uk/sightandsound/review/68263

Ogle, Connie. 'Review of *The Cabin in the Woods*.' *Miami Herald* (11 April 2012). https://www.miamiherald.com/miami-com/things-to-do/article225908795.html

Olsen, Mark. '*Cabin in the Woods* Can't See the Forest for the Trees.' *Village Voice* (11 April 2012). https://www.villagevoice.com/2012/04/11/cabin-in-the-woods-cant-see-the-forest-for-the-trees/

Paik, Peter Y. 'Apocalypse of the Therapeutic: *The Cabin in the Woods* and the Death of Mimetic Desire.' *Mimesis, Movies, and Media: Violence, Desire, and the Sacred*. Ed. Scott Cowdell, Chris Fleming and Joel Hodge. London: Bloomsbury, 2015. 105–16.

Parker, J. Ryan. 'As It Ever Was… So Shall It Never Be: Penal Substitutionary Atonement Theory and Violence in *The Cabin in the Woods*.' *Joss Whedon and Religion: Essays on an Angry Atheist's Explorations of the Sacred*. Ed. Anthony R. Mills, John W. Morehead, and J. Ryan Parker. Jefferson, NC: McFarland, 2013. 196–212.

Parrish, Jaclyn S. 'People vs. Humanity: Utilitarianism and Genre Critique in *The Cabin in the Woods*.' *Slayage: The Journal of Whedon Studies* 15.1 [45] (Winter/Spring 2017). https://www.whedonstudies.tv/uploads/2/6/2/8/26288593/parrish_slayage_15.1.pdf

Pascale, Amy. '*The Cabin in the Woods*.' *Joss Whedon: The Biography*. Chicago: Chicago Review P, 2014. 319–28.

Paul, William. *Laughing, Screaming: Modern Hollywood Horror and Comedy*. New York: Columbia UP, 1994.

Peckinpah, Sam (dir.). *Straw Dogs*. Feature Film. American Broadcasting Company (1971).

Persall, Steve. 'Audacious, Entertaining *Cabin in the Woods* Goes Over the Edge.' *Tampa Bay Times* (11 April 2012).

Petridis, Sotiris. *The Anatomy of the Slasher Film: A Theoretical Analysis*. Jefferson, NC: McFarland, 2019.

Pheasant-Kelly, Fran. 'Reframing Parody and Intertextuality in *Scream*: Formal and Theoretical Approaches to the "Postmodern" Slasher.' *Style and Form in the Hollywood Slasher Film*. Ed. Wickham Clayton. Houndmills, Basingstoke: Palgrave Macmillan, 2015. 149–60.

Phillips, Kendall R. 'A Certain Tendency in Post-Occupy Cinema: *The Cabin in the Woods, The Purge,* and *Snowpiercer.*' *A Cinema of Hopelessness: The Rhetoric of Rage in 21st Century Popular Culture*. Cham: Springer International Publishing, 2021. 15–40.

Phillips, Kendall R. 'A Certain Tendency in Post-Occupy Cinema—Nights of Horror.' *YouTube* Talk (29 October 2020). https://www.youtube.com/watch?v=-UUkNUEBObE

Phillips, Michael. '*Cabin in the Woods* Provides Snark and Scares: *Buffy* Alumni Craft a Horror Homage with Power to Surprise.' *Chicago Tribune* (12 April 2012).

Phipps, Keith. 'Interview: *The Cabin in the Woods* Director Drew Goddard.' *AV Club* (13 April 2012). https://film.avclub.com/the-cabin-in-the-woods-director-drew-goddard-1798230896

Phipps, Keith. 'Review of *The Cabin in the Woods*.' *AV Club* (12 April 2012). https://film.avclub.com/the-cabin-in-the-woods-1798172361

Pierce, Charles B. (dir.). *The Town That Dreaded Sundown*. Feature Film. American International Pictures (1976).

Pinedo, Isabel Cristina. 'Postmodern Elements of the Contemporary Horror Film.' *The Horror Film*. Ed. Stephen Prince. New Brunswick: Rutgers UP, 2004. 85–117.

Pols, Mary. 'The Cabin in the Woods: Burning Down the House of Horror.' Time (11 April 2012). https://www.metacritic.com/critic/mary-pols?page=3

Poole, W. Scott. '"I'm sorry I… ended the world": Eschatology, Nihilism and Hope in The Cabin in the Woods.' Joss Whedon and Religion: Essays on an Angry Atheist's Explorations of the Sacred. Ed. Anthony R. Mills, John W. Morehead and J. Ryan Parker. Jefferson, NC: McFarland, 2013. 213–26.

Proyas, Alex (dir.). Knowing. Feature Film. Lionsgate Films (2009).

Puig, Claudia. 'Cabin in the Woods Opens New Doors to Horror.' USA Today (12 April 2012). https://www.metacritic.com/critic/claudia-puig?page=17

Raimi, Sam (dir). The Evil Dead. Feature Film. New Line Cinema (1981).

Renner, Karen J. 'Generational Conflict, Twenty-first Century Horror Films and The Cabin in the Woods.' The Millennials on Film and Television: Essays on the Politics of Popular Culture. Ed. Betty Kaklamanidou and Margaret Tally. Jefferson, NC: McFarland, 2014. 110–25.

'Reviews and Ratings for The Cabin in the Woods.' IMDb. https://www.imdb.com/title/tt1259521/reviews?ref_=tt_urv

Rich, Katey. 'Review of The Cabin in the Woods.' Cinema Blend (May 2016). https://www.cinemablend.com/reviews/Cabin-Woods-5775.html

Richardson, Jared. 'The Horror of "Us": Nihilistic Conceptions of Humanity in The Cabin in the Woods.' MA Thesis (Emory University, 2015).

Romero, George A. (dir.). Dawn of the Dead. Feature Film. Dawn Associates (1978).

Romero, George A. (dir.). Night of the Living Dead. Feature Film. Image Ten (1968).

Rooney, David. 'Review of The Cabin in the Woods.' Hollywood Reporter (9 March 2012): 418.

Rosen, Christopher. '"Cabin in the Woods" Spoilers: Village Voice and New York Observer Reveal Key Plot Points in Reviews.' The Huffington Post (12 April 2012). https://www.huffingtonpost.co.uk/entry/cabin-in-the-woods-spoilers-village-voice-observer_n_1419326

Ross, Gary (dir.). The Hunger Games. Feature Film. Lionsgate Films (2012).

Roth, Eli (dir.). *Cabin Fever*. Feature Film. Lionsgate Films (2002).

Rowling, J. K. *Harry Potter and the Philosopher's Stone*. London: Bloomsbury, 1997.

Russell, Chuck (dir.). *The Blob*. Feature Film. TriStar Pictures (1988).

Salva, Victor (dir.). *Jeepers Creepers*. Feature Film. United Artists (2001).

Sannwald, Daniela. 'Vorwort oder: Schwarz und Weiß: Ästhetik und Moral in Michael Hanekes Werk.' *Film-Konzepte 21: Michael Haneke* (February 2011): 3–15.

Schoenbrun, Dan. 'A Conversation with *Cabin in the Woods* Director Drew Goddard.' www.filmmakermagazine.com/news/2012/04/a-conversation-with-cabin-in-the-woods-director-drew-goddard/

Schwarzbaum, Lisa. 'Review of *The Cabin in the Woods*.' *Entertainment Weekly* (23 April 2012). https://ew.com/article/2012/04/23/cabin-woods/

Scott, A. O. 'Taking a Chain Saw to Horror Movie Clichés.' *The New York Times* (12 April 2012). https://www.nytimes.com/2012/04/13/movies/the-cabin-in-the-woods-by-drew-goddard-and-joss-whedon.html

Scott, Ridley (dir.). *Alien*. Feature Film. Twentieth Century Fox (1979).

Scott, Ridley (dir.). *Blade Runner*. Feature Film. Warner Bros (1982).

Serrador, Narciso Ibáñez (dir.). *¿Quién puede matar a un niño?* Feature Film. Penta Films (1976).

Sessarego, Carrie. 'Watching the Whore: The Treatment of Jules in *The Cabin in the Woods*.' *After the Avengers: From Joss Whedon's Hottest, Newest Franchises to the Future of the Whedonverse*. Ed. Valerie Estelle Frankel. *PopMatters* (2015).

Sharkey, Betsy. '*Cabin in the Woods* Is Joss Whedon's Inside Joke.' *Los Angeles Times* (13 April 2012). https://www.latimes.com/entertainment/la-xpm-2012-apr-13-la-et-cabin-in-the-woods-20120413-story.html

Sharrett, Christopher. 'The Problem of *Saw*: "Torture Porn" and the Conservatism of Contemporary Horror Films.' *Cineaste* 35/1 (2009): 32–7.

Smith, Murray. *Engaging Characters: Fiction, Emotion, and the Cinema*. Oxford: Clarendon P, 1995.

Starr, Michael. 'Whedon's Great Glass Elevator: Space, Liminality, and Intertext in *The Cabin in the Woods*.' *Slayage: The Journal of Whedon Studies* 36/37 (Fall 2013/Winter 2014). https://www.whedonstudies.tv/uploads/2/6/2/8/26288593/starr_slayage_10.2-11.1.pdf

Stephenson, Sophie. 'Deconstructing the Gaze and Desensitisation in *The Cabin in the Woods*.' MA Thesis (Napier University, 2013).

Sterba, Wendy. 'Oh, the Horror: *Cabin in the Woods* and *Super 8*.' *J. J. Abrams vs. Joss Whedon: Duel for Media Master of the Universe*. Lanham, MD: Rowman & Littlefield, 2016. 143–72.

Stevens, Dana. '*Cabin in the Woods:* Joss Whedon's Movie Has Twisted Fun With Slasher Clichés.' *Slate* (12 April 2012). https://slate.com/gdpr?redirect_uri=%2Farticles%2Farts%2Fmovies%2F2012%2F04%2Fcabin_in_the_woods_reviewed_with_no_spoilers_.html%3Fvia%3Dgdpr-consent&redirect_host=http%3A%2F%2Fwww.slate.com

Sulistyorini, Muchamad. 'The Symbolism of Sacrificial Ritual in Drew Goddard's Film *The Cabin in the Woods*.' MA Thesis (Universitas Dian Nuswantoro Semarang, 2017).

Syder, Andrew. 'Knowing the Rules: Postmodernism and Horror Film.' *Spectator* 22/2 (Fall 2002): 78–88.

Taylor, Drew. 'SXSW '12 Interview: Drew Goddard Talks His Inspiration for "Cabin In The Woods," Working With Joss Whedon & J. J. Abrams & More.' *IndieWire* (9 March 2012). https://www.indiewire.com/2012/03/sxsw-12-interview-drew-goddard-talks-his-inspiration-for-cabin-in-the-woods-working-with-joss-whedon-j-j-abrams-more-253460/

Thacker, Eugene. *In the Dust of This Planet: Horror of Philosophy*. Ropley: Zero Books, 2011.

Tol, M. J. '"It's dangerous out there… Let's split up!": An Analysis of the Representation of the Classical Horror Film Formula in Contemporary Horror Film.' BA Thesis (Universiteit Utrecht, 2013).

Travers, Peter. 'Review of *The Cabin in the Woods*.' *Rolling Stone* (12 April 2012). https://www.rollingstone.com/movies/movie-reviews/the-cabin-in-the-woods-122574/

Uncle Creepy. 'The Cabin in the Woods—Win the Coolest Prize Pack EVER!' *Dread Central* (9 April 2012). http://www.dreadcentral.com/contests/32606/contest-closed-the-cabin-in-the-woods-win-the-coolest-prize-pack-ever/

Vary, Adam B. 'A Conversation with Joss Whedon.' *SXSW 2012*. https://schedule.sxsw.com/2012/events/event_IAP100611

Vary, Adam B. 'SXSW: *Cabin in the Woods* Kills at Premiere. Just Don't Talk About It!' *Entertainment Weekly* (10 March 2012). https://ew.com/article/2012/03/10/sxsw-cabin-in-the-woods-premiere/

Venezia, Tony. 'The Cabin in the Woods.' *Science Fiction Film and Television* 6/3 (2013): 411–15.

Verhoeven, Paul (dir.). *Basic Instinct*. Feature Film. TriStar Pictures (1992).

Vineyard, Jennifer. 'Joss Whedon on *Cabin in the Woods*, *The Avengers*, and *Nude Blondes*.' *Vulture.com* (16 April 2012). https://www.vulture.com/2012/04/joss-whedon-on-the-avengers-and-nude-blondes.html

Wagner, Katherine A. '"Haven't We Been Here Before?" *The Cabin in the Woods*, the Horror Genre, and Placelessness.' *Slayage: The Journal of Whedon Studies* 36/37 (Fall 2013/Winter 2014). https://www.whedonstudies.tv/uploads/2/6/2/8/26288593/wagner_slayage_10.2-11.1.pdf

Wallace, Lewis. 'Review: *Cabin in the Woods* Rips Horror a New One.' *Wired* (13 April 2012). https://www.wired.com/2012/04/review-cabin-in-the-woods/

Wayans, Keenen Ivory (dir.). *Scary Movie*. Feature Film. Dimension Films (2000).

'We Are Not Who We Are: Making *The Cabin in the Woods*.' *The Cabin in the Woods* (dir. Drew Goddard). Bonus Feature. Lionsgate, 2011. DVD.

Weyant, Curtis A. 'Exploring Cabins in the Whedonverse Woods.' *Slayage: The Journal of Whedon Studies* 38/39 (Summer 2014). https://www.whedonstudies.tv/uploads/2/6/2/8/26288593/weyant_slayage_11.2-12.1.pdf

Wheatley, Catherine. *Michael Haneke's Cinema: The Ethic of the Image*. New York: Berghahn Books, 2009.

Whedon, Joss. 'Afterword.' *The Cabin in the Woods: The Official Visual Companion*. London: Titan, 2012. 172–3.

Whedon, Joss. 'Let's Watch a Girl Get Beaten to Death.' *Whedonesque.com* (20 May 2007). http://whedonesque.com/comments/13271

Whedon, Joss, and Drew Goddard. *The Cabin in the Woods: The Official Visual Companion*. London: Titan, 2012.

Whedon, Joss, and Drew Goddard. 'The Screenplay.' *The Cabin in the Woods: The Official Visual Companion*. London: Titan, 2012.

Whedon, Joss, Drew Goddard and Abbie Bernstein. 'Into the Woods: Joss Whedon and Drew Goddard on the Making of the Film.' *The Cabin in the Woods: The Official Visual Companion*. London: Titan, 2012. 8–43.

Whitty, Stephen. 'A Jock, a Nerd and a Virgin Walk into a "Cabin in the Woods."' *Newark Star-Ledger* (13 April 2012). https://www.nj.com/entertainment/movies/2012/04/the_cabin_in_the_woods_review.html

Williams, Clifford. *Free Will and Determinism: A Dialogue*. Indianapolis: Hackett, 1980.

Woerner, Meredith. 'Why *Cabin in the Woods* Really Is Like a Very Special *Buffy* Episode.' *io9.com* (12 April 2012). https://io9.gizmodo.com/why-cabin-in-the-woods-really-is-like-a-very-special-bu-5901458

Woofter, Kristopher Karl. 'Watchers in the Woods: Meta-Horror, Genre Hybridity, and Reality TV Critique in *The Cabin in the Woods*.' *Reading Joss Whedon*. Ed. Rhonda V.Wilcox, Tanya R. Cochran, Cynthea Masson and David Lavery. Syracuse: Syracuse UP, 2014. 268–79.

Woofter, Kristopher Karl, and Jasie Stokes. 'Once More into the *Woods*: An Introduction and Provocation.' *Slayage: The Journal of Whedon Studies* 36/37 (Fall 2013/Winter 2014). https://www.whedonstudies.tv/uploads/2/6/2/8/26288593/woofter_stokes_slayage_10.2-11.1.pdf

Wright, Benjamin. 'Exclusive: Drew Goddard Reveals the 5 Films that Influenced "The Cabin in the Woods."' *IndieWire* (18 September 2012). https://www.indiewire.com/2012/09/exclusive-drew-goddard-reveals-the-5-films-that-influenced-the-cabin-in-the-woods-251012/

Wurmitzer, Gabriele. '"What Goes Without Saying": Michael Haneke's Confrontation with Myths in *Funny Games*.' *New Austrian Film*. Ed. Robert von Dassanowsky and Oliver C. Speck. New York: Berghahn, 2011. 166–76.

Zenco, Micah. 'The Myth of the Indispensable Nation.' *Foreign Policy* (6 November 2014). https://foreignpolicy.com/2014/11/06/the-myth-of-the-indispensable-nation/

www.ingramcontent.com/pod-product-compliance
Lightning Source LLC
Chambersburg PA
CBHW061418300426
44114CB00015B/1979